GERMANY 1919-1945

Published by CGP

Contributors:
David Barnes
Erik Blakely
Rene Cochlin
Paddy Gannon
Robert Gibson
Luke von Kotze
Keith A Mallinson
John Pritchard
Katherine Reed
Glenn Rogers
Hayley Thompson

With thanks to Hugh Mascetti and Andy Park for the proofreading.
Thanks to John Pritchard and Mark Craster-Chambers for reviewing.
Thanks to Laura Jakubowski for the copyright research.

Acknowledgements:

Page 7: 'Old Bear' medicine man of the Mandan Tribe, from a painting of 1832 (colour litho) by Catlin, George (1794-1872) (after) Private Collection / Peter Newark American Pictures / The Bridgeman Art Library Nationality / copyright status: American / out of copyright

Page 11: Pioneer family with their sodhouse, Nebraska 1889 (b/w photo) by American Photographer (19th century) Private Collection / Peter Newark American Pictures / The Bridgeman Art Library Nationality / copyright status: American / out of copyright

Page 12: Panning for Gold in the American West (b/w photo) by American Photographer (19th century) Private Collection / Peter Newark American Pictures / The Bridgeman Art Library Nationality / copyright status: American / out of copyright

Page 41: With thanks to Science Photo Library for permission to use image.

Page 72: Street urchins in Lambeth (b/w photo) by English Photographer (19th century) Private Collection / The Stapleton Collection / The Bridgeman Art Library Nationality / copyright status: English / out of copyright

Page 91: Nazi propaganda poster, 1935 (colour litho) by German School (20th century) Private Collection / Peter Newark Historical Pictures / The Bridgeman Art Library Nationality / copyright status: German / copyright unknown

Page 95: Jewish shop 1933, Mary Evans Picture Library

Every effort has been made to locate copyright holders and obtain permission to reproduce sources. For those sources where it has been difficult to trace the originator of the work, we would be grateful for information. If any copyright holder would like us to make an amendment to the acknowledgements, please notify us and we will gladly update the book at the next reprint. Thank you.

ISBN: 978 1 84762 281 5

Groovy website: www.cgpbooks.co.uk
Printed by Elanders Ltd, Newcastle upon Tyne.
Clipart sources: CorelDRAW® and VECTOR.

Important Dates

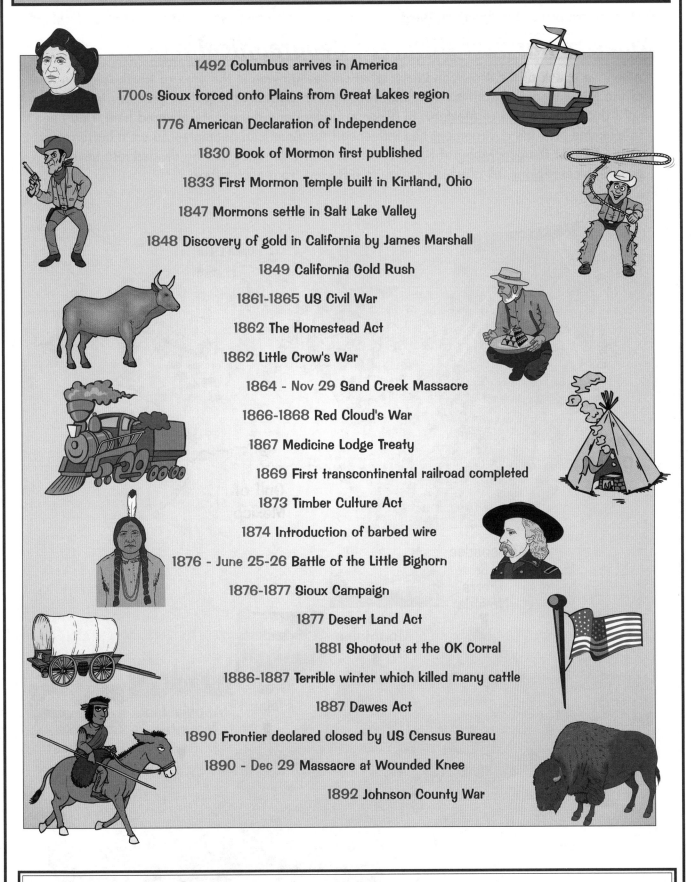

1492 Columbus arrives in America

1700s Sioux forced onto Plains from Great Lakes region

1776 American Declaration of Independence

1830 Book of Mormon first published

1833 First Mormon Temple built in Kirtland, Ohio

1847 Mormons settle in Salt Lake Valley

1848 Discovery of gold in California by James Marshall

1849 California Gold Rush

1861-1865 US Civil War

1862 The Homestead Act

1862 Little Crow's War

1864 - Nov 29 Sand Creek Massacre

1866-1868 Red Cloud's War

1867 Medicine Lodge Treaty

1869 First transcontinental railroad completed

1873 Timber Culture Act

1874 Introduction of barbed wire

1876 - June 25-26 Battle of the Little Bighorn

1876-1877 Sioux Campaign

1877 Desert Land Act

1881 Shootout at the OK Corral

1886-1887 Terrible winter which killed many cattle

1887 Dawes Act

1890 Frontier declared closed by US Census Bureau

1890 - Dec 29 Massacre at Wounded Knee

1892 Johnson County War

Welcome to the West...

Here are some dates for you to <u>remember</u> — it really is worth learning them so you get a sense of how all the events fit together.

Geographical Regions

Right, the history of the <u>American West</u>. I suppose a pretty map would be a good place to start.

America has very different Geographical regions

When we speak of the American West, what we really mean is the area of North America west of the <u>Mississippi River</u>. This river runs from the northernmost region of present-day USA, right down to the <u>Gulf of Mexico</u>. In order to understand the events covered here, you need to examine how the <u>environment</u> has influenced the American people — so we'd better start with a look at the <u>geography</u> of North America. North America can be divided into several geographical <u>regions</u>, all of which are quite <u>different</u> from each other:

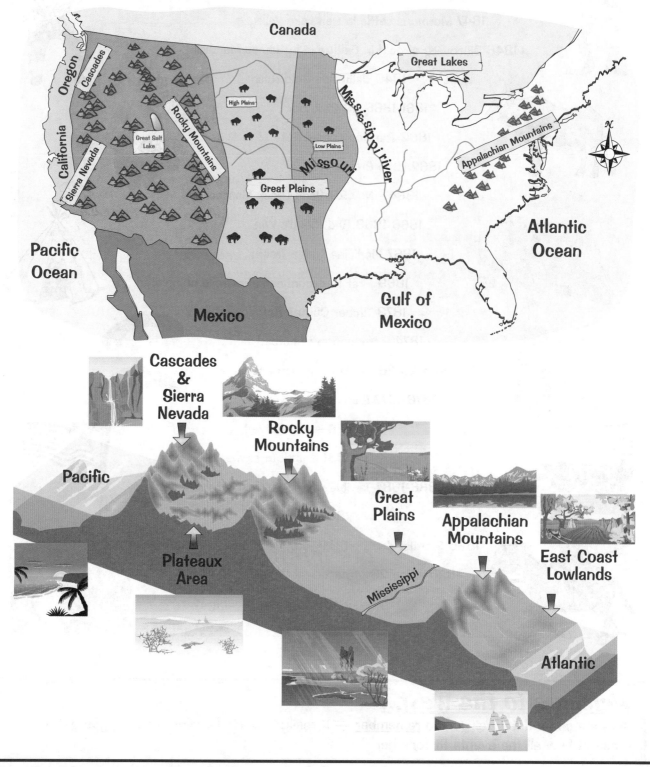

The West and its Climate

Enough of the maps. Let's talk about the weather.

The Great Plains lie in the Centre of North America

1) Central North America is dominated by the <u>Great Plains</u>.
2) The Plains are mostly a huge, flat, expanse of <u>grassland</u>. There are two bits:
   — the "<u>Low Plains</u>" to the east, with long grass (remember <u>L</u> for <u>L</u>ow and <u>L</u>ong).
   — the "<u>High Plains</u>" to the west, with short grass.
3) The Great Plains become <u>drier</u> and more desert-like the further <u>south</u> you go.

The Weather on the Plains is Extreme and scary

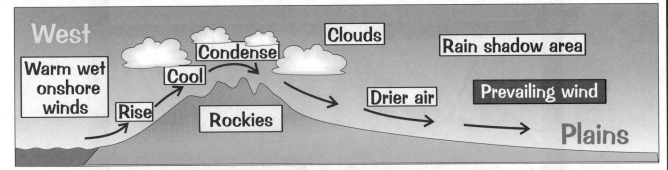

1) The <u>weather</u> across the Great Plains varies severely — it can make farming difficult even today.
2) The <u>mountains</u> on either side of the Plains produce <u>rain shadows</u> (regions with little rain). You often get <u>droughts</u> in the summer and <u>severe snow</u> in the winter.
3) Being so far from the sea means there's a huge <u>difference in temperature</u> between summer and winter.
4) <u>Tornadoes</u> are quite common — like the one that damaged Oklahoma City in 1999.
5) These extremes are described as a <u>continental climate</u>. By comparison Britain is never very far from the sea and has fairly even temperatures and mild weather — an example of a <u>temperate climate</u>.

The Rocky Mountains form a Barrier across America

1) The <u>slopes</u> on either side of the Rockies are <u>heavily wooded</u> — especially in the South.
2) Towards the centre of the Rockies is the <u>Plateaux region</u>. This is relatively flat and contains areas of <u>desert</u>. Water can run onto the Plateaux region and get trapped, only escaping by <u>evaporation</u>. This has led to the <u>Great Salt Lake</u> — important later on.

The Pacific Coastlands are milder and fertile

1) West beyond the Sierra Nevada mountains lie the <u>Pacific coastlands</u>.
2) This land is mainly <u>fertile</u>. It has a temperate climate because it is close to the sea.
3) This region was a much sought-after place to live. It still is, despite the <u>earthquake risk</u>.

You'd better learn the geography — or you're history...

OK, so you thought you were studying <u>history</u>. The thing is though, so much of what happened in the West was related to the <u>geography</u>. That means things'll make much more <u>sense</u> and be easier to remember if you get a sense of the geography first.

Maps and Dates

Here's where the main Plains Indian <u>tribes</u> lived in <u>1840</u>, the start of the study period.

<u>The Plains Indians had many different Tribes</u>

<u>Native Americans</u> used to be more commonly known as <u>American Indians</u> or the <u>Plains Indians</u>. You can blame <u>Columbus</u> for that — he thought he'd reached <u>India</u> when he first got to America in <u>1492</u>. He soon realised he hadn't, but called the people Indians anyway. A slight lack of imagination there, I'd say.

The Plains Indians weren't a single group with a single culture — there were many different tribes.

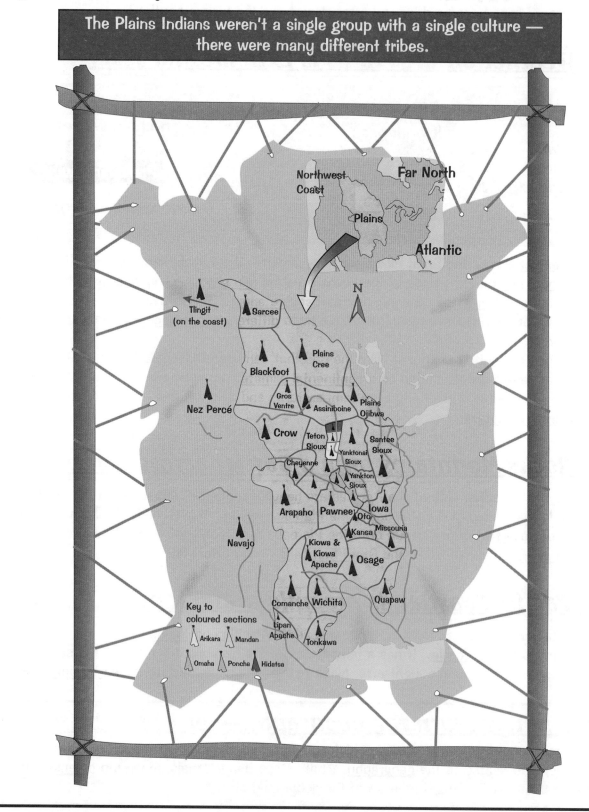

Lifestyles of the Native Americans

The Plains Indians were well <u>adapted</u> to their environment.

The Plains Indians Relied on the Buffalo

1) <u>Millions</u> of buffalo <u>grazed</u> on the <u>Plains</u> in the days before the mass slaughter of the 1870s.
2) Many Plains Indians were nomadic hunter gatherers — they <u>followed</u> the <u>buffalo</u> on its seasonal migrations. The buffalo provided the <u>necessities of life</u> —

- <u>Meat</u>.
- <u>Skins</u> for wool, clothing, shoes, harness, vessels, tents.
- <u>Sinews</u> for thread, ropes, bowstrings.
- <u>Bones</u> for implements.
- <u>Dung</u> for fuel.

3) Only along the river valleys and on the margins of the plains was there <u>some agriculture</u>.

The Horse increased the tribes' Power and Efficiency

1) The lives of the Native Americans were transformed by the <u>horse</u>, brought over by Europeans in the 16th century. It became much <u>easier to hunt</u>, and to <u>transport</u> stored food and other belongings.
2) Nomadic tribes, being scattered, were less vulnerable than farmers to <u>epidemics</u> of <u>European diseases</u>. Smallpox and cholera hit Native American farming populations hard, whereas the <u>nomadic population increased</u> to about 200 000 by 1850.
3) Tribal boundaries were <u>changeable</u>. There was a <u>gradual</u> south-westwards <u>movement</u> by the more powerful tribes — <u>Sioux</u> in the North, <u>Comanche</u> in the South — driving off weaker tribes as they advanced.

There were Differences between the Tribes

1) The <u>Sioux</u> had nomadic origins in Minnesota, while the <u>Cheyenne</u> had been farmers before they abandoned agriculture and moved onto the Plains from the east. The <u>Mandans</u>, although they hunted buffalo, never became nomads — they farmed and lived in permanent villages.
2) <u>Hereditary leadership</u> was more common in tribes which were, or had recently been, agricultural. Leadership changed <u>more flexibly</u> among long-standing nomads like the Sioux.
3) Beyond the Great Plains other Native American tribes had different cultures. Tribes in the far west (California and Oregon), such as the <u>Tlingits</u>, relied heavily on craft and trade. In the south the <u>Navajos</u> became successful shepherds after the introduction of sheep and goats.

More tribes and tribulations — if only life were simple...

You don't need to know all the tribes, but learning a <u>few</u> would be really handy — so long as you <u>spell them right</u>. And while you're learning that, a few facts about their <u>way of life</u> wouldn't go amiss. Finally, the <u>buffalo</u> aren't really buffalo — they're <u>bison</u>.

Lifestyles of the Native Americans

Understanding the <u>society</u> of the Native Americans is vital to understanding why there was such a <u>clash of cultures</u> when the settlers arrived.

Land was never Privately Owned

The idea that you could "buy" and "sell" land was meaningless to wandering tribes. <u>Land was free</u>, like air. Even to more settled tribes, <u>agriculture was a communal activity</u> — anyone could grow corn on any part of the tribal land.

Generosity was expected within the Tribe

1) Plains Indians were highly <u>individualistic</u> and cherished <u>fine possessions</u> — but didn't accumulate more than they could use.
2) <u>Generosity</u> to those in need was expected of those who could provide it, and it added to their <u>prestige and power</u>. Chiefs who weren't generous lost their <u>influence</u>.

Most men were Warriors

1) Tribal <u>warfare</u> was part of the culture of many Native Americans. Low intensity warfare and <u>raiding</u> for animals and captives was a part of life and the usual way for men to gain <u>prestige</u>.
2) "<u>Counting coup</u>" meant riding up to an enemy and merely touching him with a special stick, then getting away. Such <u>symbolic acts of bravery</u> reduced the need to kill or be killed — allowing warfare to be <u>sustainable</u>. War was never pretty though — death was always a risk.
3) Native Americans did not think of themselves as part of a Native American nation but as members of a <u>particular tribe</u>. Rival tribes therefore could be <u>strangers</u> and <u>enemies</u> to each other as much as to the white settlers.
4) Not all Native Americans were warlike, e.g. the <u>Pueblos</u> only fought in <u>self-defence</u>.

Women played a Separate role in the Community

<u>Hunting and war</u> were <u>men's business</u>. <u>Women</u> did not have to risk their lives hunting and fighting but they had much <u>more work</u> to do than the men —

- <u>Agriculture</u> — if any was done.
- Finding <u>food for the horses</u>, and <u>leading the packhorses</u> when the tribe was on the move.
- <u>Tanning</u> buffalo hides.
- Making <u>tipis</u> (buffalo hide lodges).
- Pounding meat into <u>pemmican</u> — a long-lasting foodstuff made from dried meat combined with fat and sometimes dried fruit.
- Making most of the <u>finished goods</u>. Women <u>owned</u> the things they made — which gave them <u>power</u>.

Buffaloads more for you to learn about Native Americans...

The Native Americans had a <u>very different view</u> of the world to the white settlers — something to keep in mind when looking at the decisions made by their leaders, and when thinking about the impact <u>changing circumstances</u> had on the tribes.

Religion and Tradition

The way Native Americans saw the world had a lot to do with their religion.

Native American Religion was closely linked to Nature

1) The Native Americans believed that humans are part of Nature and not masters over it.
2) They believed in a life-force called the Great Spirit that was present in nature. It was not a sentient (conscious) entity in the way that the god of the Jewish, Christian and Muslim faiths is. The Great Spirit could not be given human characteristics (anthropomorphised).
3) For Native Americans nature had a spiritual dimension and was therefore not just a set of commodities and resources for exploitation.

Circles and Animal Spirits were important

1) Native American beliefs emphasised the interdependence of all things — they saw all things as being connected. For this reason circles were spiritually important to them.
2) They believed that all things have spirits (part of the Great Spirit). Successful hunting relied on a sort of religious bargaining carried out through rituals including dances — as well as field craft and skill with the bow or rifle.
3) They believed even non-living things in nature like rocks and mountains had spirits. Activities like mining could easily be believed to upset the spirits.

Medicine Men had contact with the Spiritual Powers

1) "Medicine man" is the English term used to describe members of Native American tribes who were important for their connection to the power of the spirits.
2) Medicine men had strength, courage and understanding of both the visible and invisible worlds.
3) "Making medicine" meant to appeal to spirits via prayer, ritual or ceremony.

Medicine man from the Mandan tribe

Oral History means no books

1) The Native Americans did not have writing. Important ideas and histories of the tribes were passed from generation to generation by telling stories.
2) Native American oral history has a tendency to make their history seem less changeable than it really was.
3) Oral history can also be fragile. Native Americans had little immunity to the diseases settlers brought from Europe. Terrible epidemics — including smallpox, influenza and typhus — killed off many of the old people, and many stories were lost with them.

Write it down — oral bet you won't remember it...

It can be useful to compare Native American beliefs with other religions. Think of the similarities and differences. Remember — even if you think you know all these facts, you'll never know for sure until you try to write them down. Put pen to paper, and scribble everything down.

Revision Summary for Sections 1-2

Right, that's it for the geography and culture stuff. But before you plough straight into the next section, it's time for some questions. I know, I know, questions are boring. Yeah, it's all too easy to ignore stuff like this. It's all so interesting that you've just got to read the rest of the book straight away... The trouble is you'll soon forget it all if you don't go back over it. And if you forget it, you'll just have to relearn it later — frustrating and a bit of a hassle. Also, the more you learn now, the easier things'll be to learn later, because you'll be able to link new facts to the stuff you already know. So believe me, you really do want to work through these questions...

1) Which river approximately divides the "East" from the "West"?
2) Make a list of the geographical obstacles someone travelling from east of the Mississippi would face on a trip to California, before the railways arrived.
3) Describe the different vegetation found on the High Plains and the Low Plains.
4) Why is the weather on the Great Plains so much more severe than that of Britain or the American coasts?
5) Write out — with correct spelling — the names of three Native American tribes.
6) What animal was at the centre of the nomadic hunter-gatherer lifestyle of the Plains Indians?
7) What was the impact of the horse on the Plains Indians?
8) Why did most of the Plains Indians not suffer as badly from the epidemics that hit many other Native American tribes?
9) How fixed were tribal boundaries over the years?
10) Name and describe two tribes that didn't fit the hunter-gatherer stereotype.
11) What place did the warrior have in Native American culture?
12) What was 'counting coup'?
13) Name three things that Native American women were responsible for.
14) What is our place in the natural world according to traditional Native American spirituality?
15) Describe one difference between the Native American Great Spirit and the Christian god.
16) Many Native American spiritual beliefs placed great importance in circles.
    Give a reason for this.
17) Why might Native Americans have disliked mining?
18) Who were the "medicine men"?
19) Why is so little known of the history of America before the settlers arrived?

Maps and Early Explorers

European settlers first settled the <u>east coast</u> in the 1600s, but they didn't stay just there for long...

A few <u>Trails</u> crossed the mountains — but they weren't easy

Trails and Mines 1848 - 1874

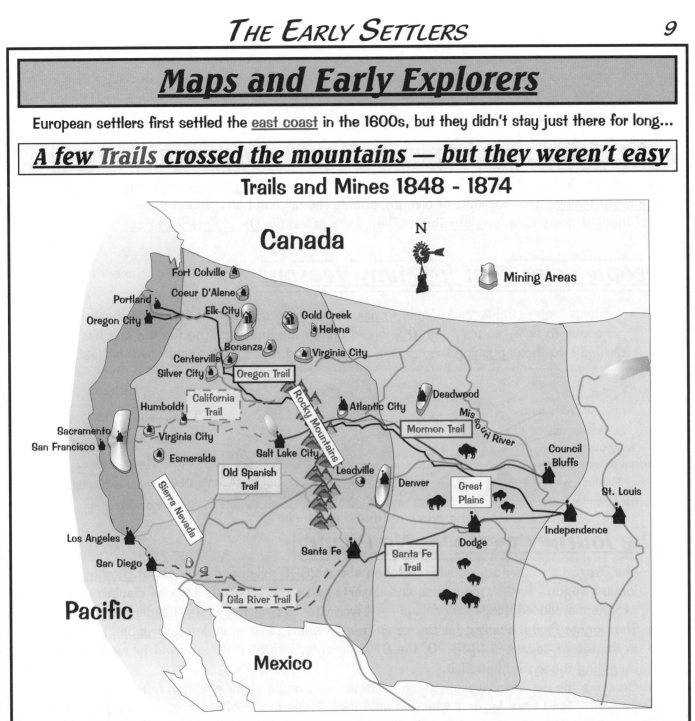

The <u>Trails</u> had been pioneered by <u>Explorers</u> and <u>Trappers</u>

1) The west coast of America first had contact with Europe via <u>Russian</u> traders in the late <u>1700s</u>. They arrived by sea and traded with the <u>Tlingit</u> Indians.

2) Explorers and trappers (known as '<u>mountain men</u>') had some knowledge of the routes that would later become the <u>Oregon</u> and <u>California</u> trails in the 1840s. In particular, the <u>South Pass</u> — the only possible route through the Rockies — was <u>first discovered</u> by mountain men.

3) Mountain men came from a variety of backgrounds, but all adopted Native American <u>survival skills</u>. Many of the mountain men took <u>Native American wives</u> — Jim Bridger had three in succession in his 40 years of wandering. Bridger was the first explorer to report the existence of the <u>Great Salt Lake</u>.

<u>Not learning these maps could coast you dearly...</u>

Another map, with lots more facts to learn. You don't of course have to be able to reproduce these perfectly, but the more <u>routes</u>, <u>places</u> and <u>events</u> you know, the more <u>sense</u> all the facts will make when you read them. Turn the page, and try <u>scribbling down</u> the map. It doesn't matter if it looks a <u>pile of tosh</u> — the main thing is to get the bits in the right places <u>relative</u> to each other.

Wagons Roll

People headed West for many different <u>reasons</u>. The journey was very <u>tough</u>.

The Plains were known as the Great American Desert

Between would-be settlers in the East and the fertile land in <u>Oregon and California</u> were <u>The Great Plains</u>. The extremes of climate, sparse rainfall and hard ground meant they were at first thought unsuitable for <u>agriculture</u>. They were called the <u>Great American Desert</u>.

People went West for Many Reasons

Many factors influenced people to <u>risk</u> the journey across America. And there needed to be — as many as <u>10%</u> would die on the journey. The factors can be divided into those <u>pushing</u> them out of the East and those <u>pulling</u> them to the West.

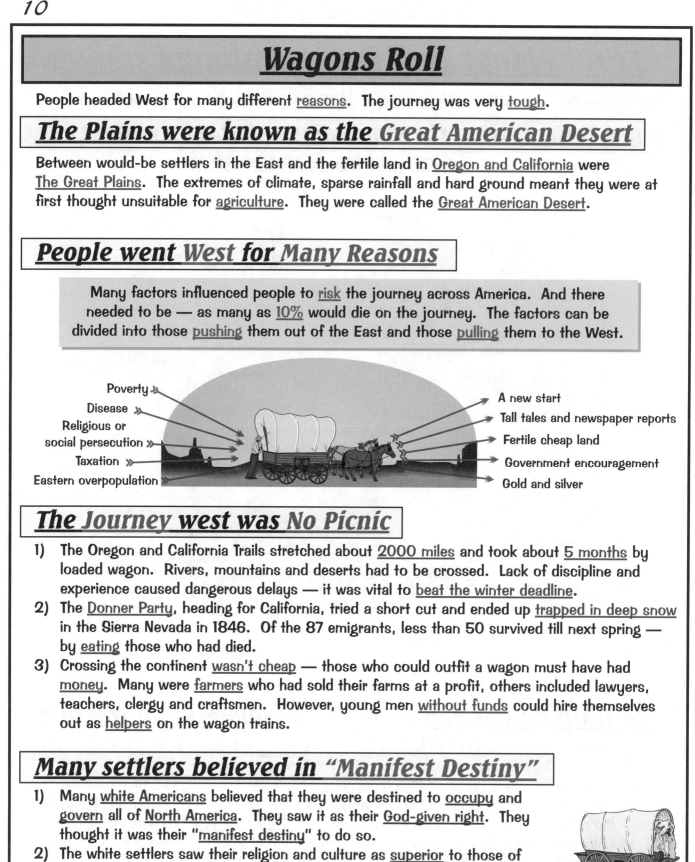

Poverty
Disease
Religious or social persecution
Taxation
Eastern overpopulation

A new start
Tall tales and newspaper reports
Fertile cheap land
Government encouragement
Gold and silver

The Journey west was No Picnic

1) The Oregon and California Trails stretched about <u>2000 miles</u> and took about <u>5 months</u> by loaded wagon. Rivers, mountains and deserts had to be crossed. Lack of discipline and experience caused dangerous delays — it was vital to <u>beat the winter deadline</u>.
2) The <u>Donner Party</u>, heading for California, tried a short cut and ended up <u>trapped in deep snow</u> in the Sierra Nevada in 1846. Of the 87 emigrants, less than 50 survived till next spring — by <u>eating</u> those who had died.
3) Crossing the continent <u>wasn't cheap</u> — those who could outfit a wagon must have had <u>money</u>. Many were <u>farmers</u> who had sold their farms at a profit, others included lawyers, teachers, clergy and craftsmen. However, young men <u>without funds</u> could hire themselves out as <u>helpers</u> on the wagon trains.

Many settlers believed in "Manifest Destiny"

1) Many <u>white Americans</u> believed that they were destined to <u>occupy</u> and <u>govern</u> all of <u>North America</u>. They saw it as their <u>God-given right</u>. They thought it was their "<u>manifest destiny</u>" to do so.
2) The white settlers saw their religion and culture as <u>superior</u> to those of the Native Americans — they saw themselves as <u>civilising the continent</u>.
3) The term "manifest destiny" was actually coined by John L. O'Sullivan in <u>1845</u> over American relations with Mexico.

A member of the westieward expansion.

More facts you're destined to learn...

There were <u>loads of reasons</u> for heading West. Make sure you can <u>list them</u>, and try to judge how important each was. For the settlers the trip was a big risk, and a leap into the unknown. If there was a <u>one in ten</u> chance that I'd die on a journey, I'd want it to be to <u>somewhere nice</u>.

Early Plains Settlers and Women's Roles

The <u>hunger for land</u> was such that the Great Plains — once known as the Great American Desert — began to be <u>settled</u>. It wasn't easy, though.

Those looking for land settled on the Plains

1) In the 1850s some settlers were on the <u>Low Plains</u> (mostly the eastern parts of <u>Kansas</u> and <u>Nebraska</u>). Settlement gradually moved along the <u>rivers</u> and onto the <u>drier lands</u> between — advancing onto lands previously <u>bypassed</u> by the wagon trains.
2) The <u>Homestead Act of 1862</u> allowed 160 acres of land <u>free to settlers</u> who occupied it for five years. And from the 1860s onwards the <u>transcontinental railways</u> (see p. 16) encouraged more settlement.

Life on the Plains Wasn't Easy

People made do

1) Houses were made of clods of turf (<u>sod houses</u>).
2) Farmers paid to borrow expensive <u>steel ploughs</u> ("<u>sod busters</u>") for the first and hardest breaking of the prairie soil.
3) <u>Dried buffalo dung</u> and <u>cow-pats</u> were used as fuel, and recycling produced an American icon — the <u>patchwork quilt</u>.

Pioneer family with their sod house in Nebraska, 1889

Conditions were very difficult

1) There was <u>little or no wood</u> for building or fuel.
2) The land was <u>too hard</u> for light ploughs.
3) On the High Plains <u>lack of water</u> meant crops like maize failed, and <u>wells</u> had to be dug a hundred feet deep or more.
4) <u>Wind</u> and <u>extremes</u> of climate battered, froze and baked the land in turn. <u>Grasshopper plagues</u> often destroyed crops.

Life for Women on the Plains was a Struggle

1) Women settlers worked side by side with men in the struggle to establish new farms — so they took part in much <u>more decision-making</u> than women in Europe or the East of America.
2) They were also largely responsible for <u>housework</u> and the <u>education of their children</u>.
3) They maintained <u>gardens</u>, looked after <u>animals</u> and made <u>household necessities</u> and goods such as clothing, soap, tallow candles, bread, biscuits, butter and cheese.
4) Another problem was the <u>loneliness</u> of the prairie. Women combated the isolation. They nursed the sick and helped each other in childbirth. Forming church groups and other <u>social networks</u>, they helped <u>civilise</u> the frontier.

Settle down — it's time to ex-plain yourself...

Life on the Plains for the settlers was a real struggle. Only those who were able to <u>adapt</u> — and who were lucky enough to avoid disaster — could prosper. It's worth remembering just how <u>tough</u> it was, and how small the margin between success and failure.

The Gold Rush

The discovery of <u>gold</u> would change the West forever.

Gold was found in California in 1848

1) Gold was found by James Marshall, working at John Sutter's sawmill in California in <u>January 1848</u> — just nine days before California changed hands from Mexico to the USA.
2) The news leaked out and people went crazy with <u>gold-fever</u>. In December <u>President Polk</u> boasted in his message to Congress of the riches to be found.
3) Soon there were <u>tens of thousands</u> of fortune-seekers coming to California — they were known as "<u>49ers</u>". During 1848-1852 the non-Native American population rose from <u>an estimated 14 000</u> to <u>about 225 000</u>. Many lived in makeshift <u>camps</u>, some of which grew into <u>mining towns</u> like Angels Camp and Placerville.
4) Some came along the settlers' trails. Others came by sea, either round <u>Cape Horn</u> or by sailing down to the <u>Isthmus of Panama</u>, crossing overland and sailing back up to California.
5) Some came to run <u>service industries</u>: store keepers, saloon owners, prostitutes — all looking for huge prices for their wares.

Not everyone made a Fortune

1) The first gold was found by <u>panning</u> the stream beds. Most people only came equipped for this method, but the streams were soon <u>exhausted</u> and expensive <u>underground mining</u> took over.
2) Prices for everything were huge, including <u>transport home</u>. Many '49ers had little choice — they could <u>work for mining companies</u> in foul conditions, or starve.

Panning for gold

There were problems with Law and Order

1) <u>Criminals</u> were attracted to the Gold Rush. There were plenty of con men, violent thieves and claim-jumpers (who stole other people's claims to successful mines).
2) Until 1866 the USA had <u>no law</u> regulating mining claims. The miners had to organize their own system for recording and defending claims.
3) They formed their own <u>miners' courts</u>. They had no permanent prisons, so <u>death sentences</u> were often carried out immediately. There was no right to appeal.
4) As some mining towns grew, committees of civic-minded people arranged for <u>full municipal government</u>.

Native Americans and the Environment suffered

1) In California the Native American population dropped from around 150 000 to <u>less than 30 000</u> during 1845-1870. This was the result of <u>violent attacks</u>, <u>epidemics</u> and being <u>driven off</u> their land.
2) Timber for mine supports used up <u>forests</u> for miles around. <u>Chemicals</u> used in mining, such as mercury, <u>polluted</u> the environment.

1849 — remember how it panned out...

The Gold Rush is a really important point in American history. The massive rush of people led to California becoming an American state in <u>1850</u> — and it only goes to show the role that <u>geography</u> (the presence of gold) and <u>chance</u> (Marshall stumbling across it) can have in history.

The Mormons

Not everyone sought gold or fertile land — the Mormons moved to escape persecution.

The Mormons also travelled West

Farmers and miners weren't the only settlers. A third group were "The Church of Jesus Christ of the Latter Day Saints" — or Mormons. This faith was started by Joseph Smith, who claimed to have seen a vision of an angel called Moroni in 1823. Moroni told Smith to find some engraved gold plates hidden on a hillside. Smith translated these engraved plates and published the translations in the Book of Mormon in 1830. It told how Jesus had visited America after the Resurrection, and also how three of the lost tribes of Israel had come to America, from which the Indians were descended.

Some Nineteenth-Century Mormon Beliefs and Practices

Polygamy — A man could have more than one wife.

Proselytisation — Mormons should try to convert other people to their faith.

Politics — Church leaders should seek and be given political power over Mormons and others.

Property — The church held property. There were no rights to individual ownership.

People of God — Obedience would make the Mormons God's chosen people in Heaven and on Earth.

The Mormons were Persecuted for their religion

Many aspects of the Mormons' faith didn't go down so well with other Americans:
1) Polygamy was seen as scandalous. Many thought it was as bad as slavery.
2) Their efforts to convert people raised fears of rapid expansion and annoyed non-converts.
3) Political aspirations threatened non-believers with religiously inspired legislation.
4) Some Mormons formed a militia (the Danites) and there was violence against dissenters.
5) Claims to be the chosen ones of God made the Mormons seem arrogant.
6) Individual ownership is pivotal to American culture. Ironically, working as a community made them wealthy — and this also annoyed non-Mormons.

They were Driven Out of place after place

Temple at Kirtland

1) The Mormons first settled in Kirtland, Ohio, 1831-7. Violence included J. Smith being tarred and feathered (1832). Their first temple was built here in 1833. The Mormon bank collapsed in 1837 and they were finally driven out to Missouri.
2) In Missouri the Mormons' anti-slavery stance annoyed slave-owners. The Danites were suspected of plotting with Indians. Many of the leaders were arrested — but Brigham Young emerged to lead the Mormons to Illinois.
3) Nauvoo, Illinois — A charter, given by the governor, allowed Mormons an army and laws. Smith declared his candidacy for President. In June 1844 Smith was arrested for the destruction of a dissident printing press. Later that month, he was killed in jail by an angry mob.
4) Some factions then left the Mormons, but 15 000 remained when Brigham Young took over.

Danite forget about the Mormons...

The episode of the Mormons is an important chapter in American history, so don't ignore it. The trouble is there's lots of facts to learn. The most important thing is to understand the basic features of their religion, and why these and their actions led to their persecution. Write a brief summary of the page — an ideal way to learn it.

The Mormons

Map of the Routes Taken by the Mormons

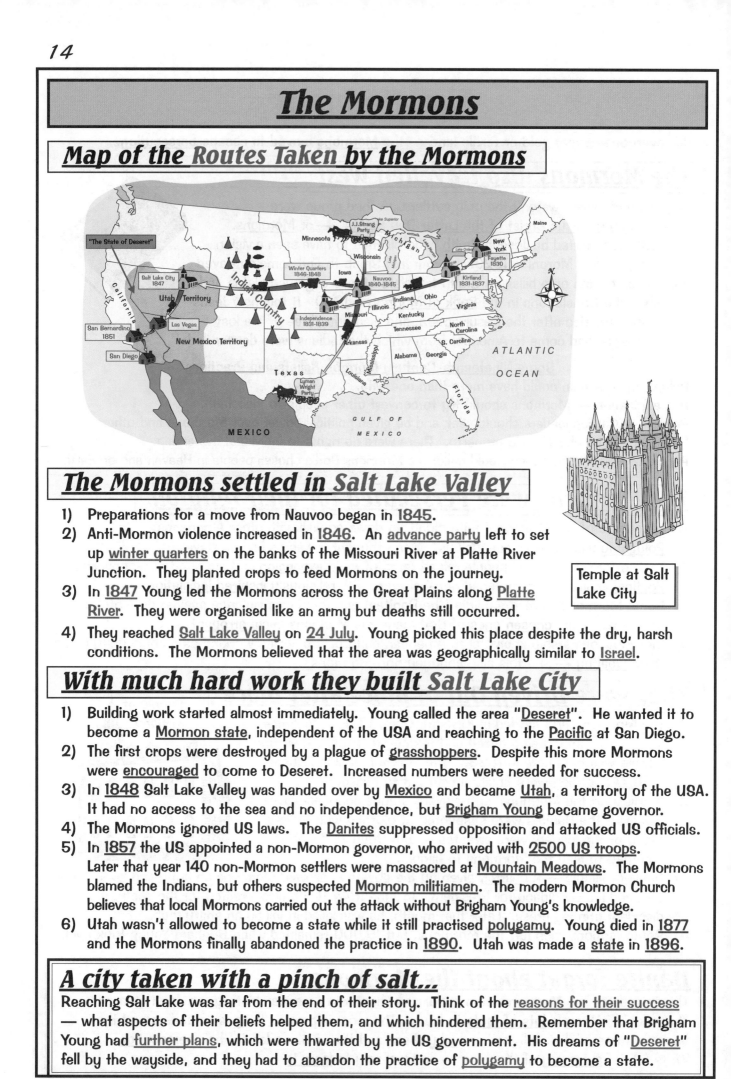

Temple at Salt Lake City

The Mormons settled in Salt Lake Valley

1) Preparations for a move from Nauvoo began in 1845.
2) Anti-Mormon violence increased in 1846. An advance party left to set up winter quarters on the banks of the Missouri River at Platte River Junction. They planted crops to feed Mormons on the journey.
3) In 1847 Young led the Mormons across the Great Plains along Platte River. They were organised like an army but deaths still occurred.
4) They reached Salt Lake Valley on 24 July. Young picked this place despite the dry, harsh conditions. The Mormons believed that the area was geographically similar to Israel.

With much hard work they built Salt Lake City

1) Building work started almost immediately. Young called the area "Deseret". He wanted it to become a Mormon state, independent of the USA and reaching to the Pacific at San Diego.
2) The first crops were destroyed by a plague of grasshoppers. Despite this more Mormons were encouraged to come to Deseret. Increased numbers were needed for success.
3) In 1848 Salt Lake Valley was handed over by Mexico and became Utah, a territory of the USA. It had no access to the sea and no independence, but Brigham Young became governor.
4) The Mormons ignored US laws. The Danites suppressed opposition and attacked US officials.
5) In 1857 the US appointed a non-Mormon governor, who arrived with 2500 US troops. Later that year 140 non-Mormon settlers were massacred at Mountain Meadows. The Mormons blamed the Indians, but others suspected Mormon militiamen. The modern Mormon Church believes that local Mormons carried out the attack without Brigham Young's knowledge.
6) Utah wasn't allowed to become a state while it still practised polygamy. Young died in 1877 and the Mormons finally abandoned the practice in 1890. Utah was made a state in 1896.

A city taken with a pinch of salt...

Reaching Salt Lake was far from the end of their story. Think of the reasons for their success — what aspects of their beliefs helped them, and which hindered them. Remember that Brigham Young had further plans, which were thwarted by the US government. His dreams of "Deseret" fell by the wayside, and they had to abandon the practice of polygamy to become a state.

Maps and Dates

The coming of the <u>railways</u> brought <u>opportunities</u> — to move West or to sell your cattle.

Map Showing _Stage Coach Routes_ <u>and</u> _Railways_

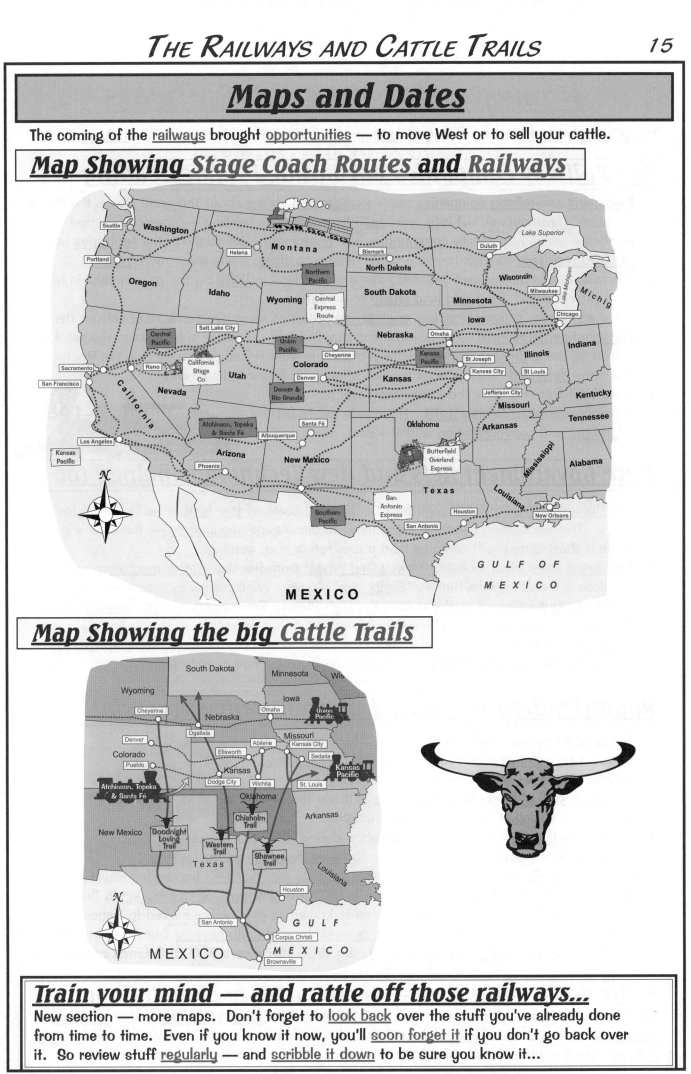

Map Showing the big _Cattle Trails_

Train your mind — and rattle off those railways...

New section — more maps. Don't forget to <u>look back</u> over the stuff you've already done from time to time. Even if you know it now, you'll <u>soon forget it</u> if you don't go back over it. So review stuff <u>regularly</u> — and <u>scribble it down</u> to be sure you know it...

Homesteaders and the Railways

The US government did a lot to encourage homesteaders and the building of the railways.

The Railway Companies encouraged Homesteading

1) Politicians and railway companies made exaggerated claims about the good life on the Plains. "Booster" (promotional) railways were built by companies trusting — correctly — that their existence would help create communities and customers. Politicians in the territories wanted 60 000 residents so their territory could become a state, giving them more power.
2) The railway companies were granted huge areas of land in 1862 by the government to help fund the railways. They sold land cheap to settlers.
3) Huge economic, geographical and engineering problems were overcome to construct the transcontinental railroad. The government supplied loans. Labour shortages in the West were solved by using Chinese workers. Steep gradients were risked when crossing the Rockies. The army defended railway gangs against attacks by Plains Indian tribes.
4) Lines built from the east and west finally met at Promontory, Utah, in May 1869. This made westward migration, and communication with the East, much easier.

More Government Acts and new Technology helped too

1) The Homestead Act of 1862 gave each settler 160 acres of free land, if he farmed it for 5 years. This occupancy condition was meant to discourage speculators — those aiming to make a short-term profit on rising land prices rather than settling.
2) New crops were tried, including Turkey Red Wheat from Russia. Better machinery was developed, including John Deere's "Sodbuster" plough. Wind pumps increased water supply.
3) New techniques allowed settlement on the High Plains. Farmers learnt "dry farming", using techniques like turning the soil after rain to retain the moisture.
4) In less fertile areas farmers needed more than 160 acres. The Timber Culture Act (1873) and the Desert Land Act (1877) gave them more land for free or at low cost.

Homesteading was hard but eventually successful

1) The failure rate for new farms was high. There were frequent droughts and problems caused by over-grazing.
2) Despite this, the Great Plains emerged as the "breadbasket" of the nation. The railways made the boom possible by linking producers to wider markets.
3) There were 10 million immigrants to America during 1865-90 — many of these helped settle the West, such as the Scandinavians on the Dakotas.
4) Some African-Americans moved West after the Civil War (1861-5) had ended slavery. When the end of post-war reconstruction in 1877 brought renewed oppression in the old South, approximately 20 000 black migrants known as exodusters moved to Kansas in 1879.
5) The Homestead Act failed to discourage speculators and drain poverty from Eastern cities, but it did achieve the settlement of the West. By 1900 there were 500 000 farms on the Plains.

Settle down at the back — there's a lot to plough through...

Being one of the first settlers sounds like a cross between a great adventure and an absolute nightmare. The promise of free land for those who could make a go of it must have been a big pull. If someone offered me a bit of land for a small farm, I'd be tempted to have a dig.

The Beef Bonanza and the Cattle Trails

The Beef Bonanza was an epic business while it lasted.

The Beef Bonanza began in Texas

1) Open ranching of cattle started in Mexico. Texas rebelled against Mexico in 1835, and joined the USA in 1845. Many Mexicans were driven out, leaving their cattle to American ranchers.

2) The Anglo-American settlers brought their own cattle with them, some descended from English Longhorns. Their cattle interbred with Mexican Criollos, producing the famous Texas Longhorn.

3) Many Texans left their ranches to fight in the Civil War (1861-1865). While they were away their cattle continued to breed. Charles Goodnight left behind 180 cattle, but returned in 1865 to find he owned 5000.

4) Increased popularity of beef in the 1850s had made it worthwhile for Texan ranchers to drive cattle northwards (where they could make more money at market).

The great Cattle Trails linked supply with demand

1) In 1860 Oliver Loving drove the first herd from Texas to Colorado. Loving died of his injuries in 1867 after a fight with Comanches, but his partner Charles Goodnight drove an even bigger herd along the Goodnight-Loving Trail in 1868 to John Iliff in Wyoming, supplying Union Pacific Railroad construction gangs.

2) There were four principal cattle trails — the Goodnight-Loving Trail, the Western Trail, the Chisholm Trail and the Shawnee Trail — see map, p.15.

3) 1871 was the peak year of the Long Drive — 600 000 cattle were driven north. Trails were between 1200 and 1500 miles long, and progress of 15 miles was considered a good day's drive. Cowboys had to contend with storms, river floods and, worst of all, stampedes.

The Cattle Trails led to the Cow Towns

1) Joseph McCoy saw money could be made by moving beef cattle by rail to the eastern cities and Indian reservations. Settlers didn't want Texas herds crossing their land, so McCoy persuaded the Union Pacific Eastern Division (later known as Kansas Pacific) to build their railroad through the remote town of Abilene (see map, p.15).

2) In sixty days in 1867 he built Abilene up to a fully equipped cow town, soon connected to Texas via the Chisholm Trail.

3) In a few years, about 3 million cattle had passed through Abilene, which was succeeded by other cow towns such as Wichita, Ellsworth and Dodge City as the railway advanced.

4) Cow towns earned a violent reputation — cowboys often went wild there after the hardships of the trail.

> Cattle ranches were also set up on the northern Great Plains. Raising the cattle was more efficient than trailing them from Texas every year. John Iliff became a powerful rancher with 35 000 cattle in Colorado and Wyoming.

Beef up your answers — learn these facts...

Although cattle still had to be transported huge distances over land to reach them, the railways were very important for getting cattle to their final destinations. Make sure you know the reasons for the rise of the cattle industry, and the role played by the trails, railways and cow towns.

The Cattle Kingdoms

The 1860s to the 1880s were the ranchers' heyday.

The Open Range supported the Cattle Kingdoms

1) Ranches on the Great Plains were "open range" — there were no fences and cattle were free to graze where they liked.
2) Herds mingled without supervision. At the spring and autumn round-up (the original "rodeo"), calves were branded with the same mark as their mothers. Breeding cows were set free for another year and steers (castrated males) set aside for the drive to the railway.

Cattlemen and Homesteaders often clashed

1) Longhorn cattle carried a tick which carried a disease called Texas Fever. The tough Longhorns were immune to it but homesteaders' cattle were not. This meant homesteaders often lost cattle when herds were driven across their land. Lack of wood for fences meant many crops were also destroyed by passing herds.

2) From 1874 the introduction of barbed wire made stock-proof fencing cheap. Homesteaders fenced their land, reducing cattlemen's access to water and making cattle drives much harder.

Changing Tastes and Hard Winters ended the Bonanza

1) Eastern markets began to demand a higher quality of meat than the Longhorn could provide. Ranchers like Iliff and Goodnight started crossbreeding Longhorns with Herefords — meatier but less resistant to harsh conditions.
2) States passed quarantine laws — from 1885 Kansas shut its borders to Texas cattle between March and November.
3) The herds became too big for the grazing areas. The over-grazed range meant underfed cattle entered the terrible winter of 1886-7 in weakened condition. Homesteaders' fences became death traps as cattle piled against them during blizzards. Average losses were perhaps 30%. Many cowboys also died.
4) Businesses which survived the 1880s economised by raising better-quality animals on smaller land units, shifting towards a more managed environment. Ranching now depended on the ability to feed livestock in winter, so dependence on irrigation increased.
5) More intensive ranching also favoured smaller scale operations — family-owned rather than corporate.
6) Ranchers, like homesteaders, now used barbed wire enclosures. Cowboys became domesticated ranch hands with the change from open range to fenced pasture.

Get a moo-ve on — there's a long way to go...

It's not just the Native Americans and settlers who didn't get on. Cattlemen and homesteaders were another two groups who came into conflict. Life on the plains was pretty tough eh?

The Real Cowboys

We all have a picture of what a cowboy should be like from the famous film versions — John Wayne, Clint Eastwood, Billy Crystal. What were they really like?

The Cowboys came from a Variety of Backgrounds

1) Large numbers of cowboys were Mexican or African Americans.
   Some were ex-soldiers from the Civil War, some were outlaws.
2) Most cowboys were young and single. They had little time for a family life.
3) A tiny number of women took to ranching in their own right.
   The Becker sisters ran a ranch in the San Luis Valley in the 1880s.

The cowboy's Job was Very Tough and Badly Paid

1) Boredom and discomfort were part of the job. Winters were spent watching the cattle from line camps on the edges of the ranch. Trail life was mostly breathing dust and staring at cows.
2) Longhorn cattle are big and aggressive. Rounding them up and cutting out the correct cattle from mixed herds on the open range took skill.
3) Indians often charged a levy for crossing their land. Sometimes Indians and other rustlers would steal or stampede cattle. Diplomacy or guns could be needed.
4) Whilst on the trail the cowboys were highly disciplined as much by each other as by their bosses. They had to work as a team to succeed and there weren't the chances to misbehave.
5) Pay was very low and tended to come in one lump at the end of a drive. Young men at the end of a difficult, boring job with money in their pockets didn't need encouragement to go wild. Cow towns like Abilene and Cheyenne grew to provide ample vices and temptations.

Cowboys needed the Tools of their Trade

Pistol — Used to shoot wolves, rustlers and (rarely) in drunken brawls. Pistols like the Colt "Peacemaker" (introduced in 1873) fired brass cartridges. They were more reliable, safer and quicker to reload than the "cap and ball" revolvers of the Civil War.

Hat — Broad-brimmed felt hat to give protection from all weathers.

Bandana — Large handkerchief worn around the neck or over the nose and mouth to protect them from dust.

Saddle — Large and with a high pommel (at the front) and cantle (at the back) for support — increasing comfort for both rider and horse. The cap on the pommel allows a rope to be tied off.

Horse — The best horse for cowboys was the American Quarter Horse. Sturdy and compact, this breed could manoeuvre well and travel all day.

Boots — The high-heeled boot originated in Mexico and helped the feet stay in the stirrups.

Chaps — Leather overtrousers that protect the legs from thorns and cattle.

Lariat or lasso — used to rope cows, especially during roundups for branding.

Stop horsing around and do some work...

There are lots of stories and legends about cowboys in the American West. The thing is though, the life of a cowboy generally bore very little relation to the legend — very few cowboy films, for instance, actually have any cows in. Think about how and why the legends grew.

Revision Summary for Sections 3-4

More questions now, I'm afraid. Don't forget though that if you haven't looked back at the previous questions on page 8 already, then it's about time you did. You really do have to keep going over stuff like this if you want it to stick in that head of yours. You should really go over these questions till you can reel off those answers — just like that. When you can do that, you'll know you know it.

1) By what name were the Great Plains also known in the 1840s?

2) What factors made early migrants want to cross America?

3) Give a brief description of "Manifest Destiny".

4) Name one technological advance that helped Plains homesteaders.

5) What made homesteading on the Plains so difficult?

6) Who first discovered gold in California?

7) a) What was the most common technique used by prospectors to find gold?
   b) This technique only worked for the early arrivals. Why?
   c) What choice faced many of the later arrivals because of this?

8) How did the expectations of the '49ers compare with reality?

9) Who kept law and order in the mining camps?

10) What is the full name of the Mormon faith and who founded it?

11) Describe the aspects of the Mormon faith that were unpopular with most other Americans.

12) Why did the Mormons decide to settle in the Salt Lake Valley?

13) What happened at Mountain Meadows?

14) Why did the railway companies encourage homesteading?

15) How did the railway companies solve their labour problems?

16) Where and when was the East-West rail link finally completed?

17) What were the special features of "dry farming"?

18) How was the Texas Longhorn bred?

19) Name one man who benefited from the change in cattle population during the Civil War, and explain how he cashed in on his good fortune.

20) How did the spread of the railways help the cattlemen?

21) Who made his fortune by building up Abilene?

22) What was "Texas Fever"?

23) Discuss the reasons for conflict between cattlemen and homesteaders.

24) Outline three factors that brought an end to the long trail drives of the Beef Bonanza.

25) Give one reason why was the "Peacemaker" was a better pistol than the ones carried during the Civil War.

26) What made the American Quarter Horse a good breed for cowboys to use?

Maps and Dates

Time for some politics. The US government was a key factor in many episodes of the American West's history, so you probably ought to know a bit about it.

1) Map Showing Annexation of Native American Land

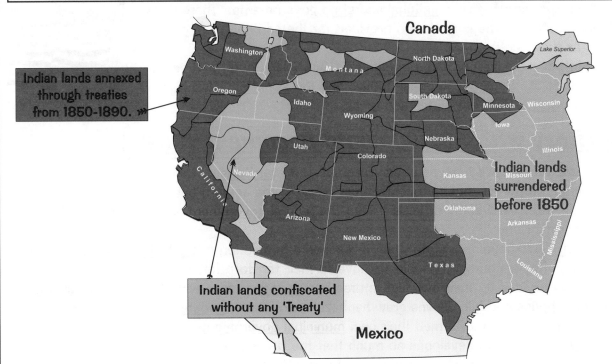

Indian lands annexed through treaties from 1850-1890. »

Indian lands surrendered before 1850

Indian lands confiscated without any 'Treaty'

2) Map of USA showing Dates of Statehood

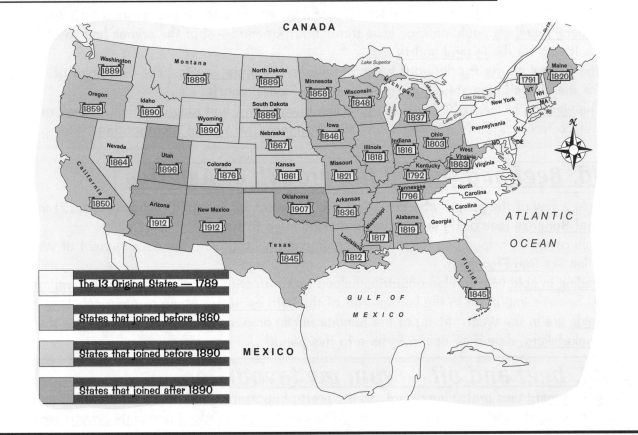

The 13 Original States — 1789

States that joined before 1860

States that joined before 1890

States that joined after 1890

Government for the People

As the US grew it brought more land and people under its system of government.

The United States has a Federal Government of States

1) The US Constitution (1787) established a federal system of government — with power split between national and state governments. There were 13 original states. The constitution provided for the addition of more states as the country grew.
2) Each state has a governor and a legislature (law-making body). It sends delegates to the House of Representatives and the Senate in Washington.
3) Laws can vary in different states and areas.

A Territory with 60,000 could become a State

1) As the West developed it was carved up roughly into territories. This is why the borders of the western states are much straighter than those of the eastern ones.
2) Territories could elect some officials — but the federal government appointed many of the more important ones.
3) A territory could become a state when it reached a population of 60 000. Ambitious local politicians often encouraged people to move to their territory for this reason.
4) States were divided by their own legislatures into counties, each with its own administrative seat, courthouse and jail. Towns grew haphazardly or were "boosted" into existence by business promoters, and formed their own municipal governments.
5) By 1890 the West had developed so much that the US Bureau of the Census declared the frontier closed. There were no new areas of empty land awaiting settlers.

Different Courts and Lawmen had different jurisdictions

1) Many town marshals only controlled law enforcement in a small area around their town.
2) Federal marshals could enforce laws throughout America — but the crimes had to be those dealt with by the federal courts.
3) The federal courts try different types of case to the state courts. The final point of appeal for the states is the state governor — not the federal courts.
4) The election of local officials made jobs like town sheriff and judge political. These men were often drawn into the violence of the "Western Civil War of Incorporation" (see p. 23).

Gold, Beef and Oil fed the growth of America

1) Only a few of the people who struggled into the West for the gold rushes (see p.12) and the Beef Bonanza (see p. 17) succeeded in making huge fortunes.
2) Gold revenues helped pay for the transcontinental railways and the development of Western cities like San Francisco.
3) Trading in gold with foreign countries helped make America a major world trading nation.
4) Oil became important in the last quarter of the 19th century. Many of America's best oil fields are in the West. Many of the famous family empires associated with oil, like the Rockefellers, date their rise in fortune to this period.

Gold, beef and oil — yum my favourite...

The government was pretty important, so it's pretty important you know a bit about it, and how it was organised. Make sure you know the difference between federal and state government.

Section Five — Politics and Law and Order

The Wild West

The Old West was a pretty violent place. You need to get to grips with the events of some of the famous clashes in the West, as well as their underlying causes.

A "Western Civil War of Incorporation" — or just lawlessness?

1) The violence in the late 1800s in the American West was partly due to changes in society.
2) Cattle barons, railroads and other corporations — using the power and influence that their size gave them — were taking over from the homesteaders, small ranchers and prospectors. Some historians call the violence it sparked the "Western Civil War of Incorporation".

3) Outlaws were treated as heroes by some for standing up for ordinary people.
4) The brutal James Younger gang, led by Jesse James, acquired a Robin Hood reputation because their victims — banks and the railway companies — were institutions hated by many.

Jesse James

- Conflicts like the Lincoln County War and the Johnson County War (see p. 24) became known as range wars — small-scale conflicts between different groups of ranchers with competing interests.
- The Lincoln County War in New Mexico, in which Billy the Kid played a part, was fought between rival cattle kings L.G. Murphy and John Chisum.

Wyatt Earp became a Lawman despite a dodgy past

1) Born in 1848, Wyatt Earp was arrested in 1871 for rustling (horse stealing) in Missouri. Rather than stand trial he fled the state, and the federal system did nothing to prevent his later career as a lawman.
2) He was a natural recruit for the forces of incorporation as he was a keen entrepreneur as well as an effective gunman.
3) He, his brothers and Doc Holliday killed two McLaurys and a Clanton at the OK Corral on 26 October 1881. The dead men were typical of the small ranchers/outlaws who opposed the growth of big business in the West. A bloody feud followed.
4) As victor, Wyatt Earp not only wrote the history of the OK Corral, but got to write the screenplay as well — he worked as an advisor on the early Hollywood westerns before he died in 1929.

Wyatt Earp

Earp also took part in the so-called Dodge City War of 1883 — a faction fight between a saloon-keeper friend of Earp and a corrupt mayor. Dodge City had a reputation as the "Wickedest City in America", but by 1886 the cattle trails had gone and Dodge had become a sleepy little town.

Learn it or lose marks — it's Earp to you...

This is what all those Western movies are about. But unlike in the Hollywood version, the lines between who was right and wrong aren't that clear. Make sure you know why big businesses clashed with small homesteaders and ranchers — and why these clashes were often violent.

The Wild West

Lawlessness was a big problem in the West. Many people took the law into their own hands.

Lack of law enforcement led to Vigilante groups

1) Early on the lack of any formal law enforcement meant that vigilante groups sprang up in places like the Gold Rush boom towns. These were made up of ordinary citizens who tried to deliver law and order — often brutally.

2) Later on vigilante groups were largely a tool of big business. They were used as a last resort against the "outlaw" groups opposing the expansion of their empires.

3) Under these circumstances justice, legality, good and evil were often a matter of debate — lawmen and criminals were often very hard to tell apart.

I hate cattle rustling.

The Johnson County War — a vigilante raid in 1892

1) Small landowners in Johnson County felt that the cattle barons were stealing their land. Ranchers thought that the homesteaders were rustling (stealing) their cattle.

In 1889 a rancher called A.J. Bothwell wanted land claimed by a storekeeper called James Averill. Averill lived with a prostitute called Ella Watson who had some rebranded cows. Bothwell accused them both of rustling and a lynch mob murdered Watson and Averill in front of their cabin. There were more murders of alleged rustlers in 1891.

2) In 1892 the Wyoming Stock Growers Association (who represented ranchers) hired gunmen and drew up a hit list of 70 suspected rustlers. They mounted a huge vigilante raid into Johnson County, calling themselves the "Regulators". The Union Pacific Railroad laid on a special train for them.

3) The Regulators killed two alleged rustlers, Nate Champion and Nick Ray, but a group of locals came out of Buffalo and laid siege to the "invaders" at a ranch called the TA.

4) More locals gathered, including Buffalo's sheriff, until there were about 250 men ready to kill the Regulators. The Stock Growers Association had influence with the government via the Republican Party and the President. They used this to call out the army, who rescued the Regulators in a bloodless truce.

5) Despite the efforts of the locals no prosecutions resulted.

County Wars — I don't know... about eight?

Make sure you understand the reasons for all the problems and conflicts — and why vigilante groups arose. Remember that backing up arguments with examples is essential in the Exams, so you really do need to learn those facts. You know the drill — turn the page and scribble...

Maps and Dates

Long-running disputes between the Native Americans and settlers finally came to a head in the Indian Wars.

There were many Battles on the Plains

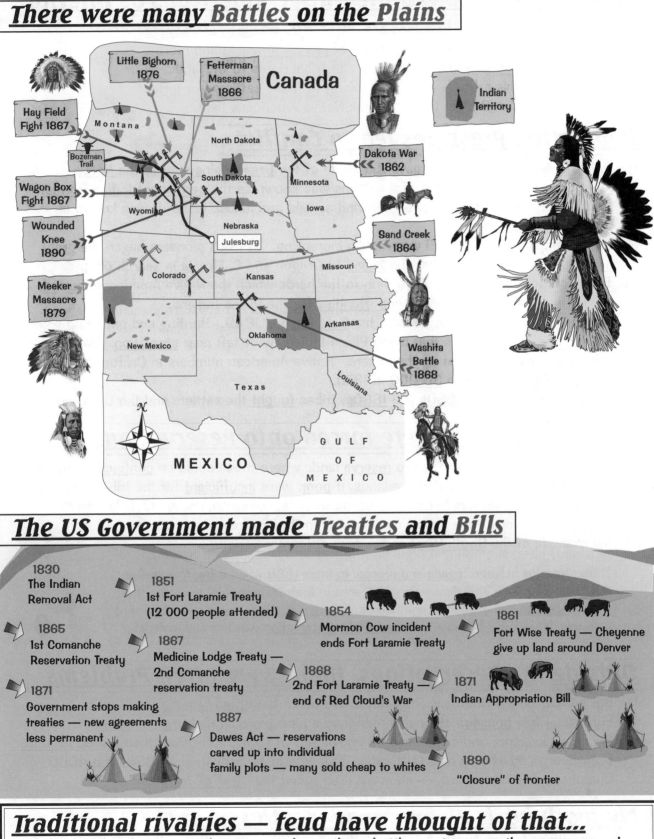

The US Government made Treaties and Bills

1830 The Indian Removal Act

1851 1st Fort Laramie Treaty (12 000 people attended)

1854 Mormon Cow incident ends Fort Laramie Treaty

1861 Fort Wise Treaty — Cheyenne give up land around Denver

1865 1st Comanche Reservation Treaty

1867 Medicine Lodge Treaty — 2nd Comanche reservation treaty

1868 2nd Fort Laramie Treaty — end of Red Cloud's War

1871 Indian Appropriation Bill

1871 Government stops making treaties — new agreements less permanent

1887 Dawes Act — reservations carved up into individual family plots — many sold cheap to whites

1890 "Closure" of frontier

Traditional rivalries — feud have thought of that...

Another very handy map. Make sure you know those battles — turn over the page now and roughly sketch the map. Remember — don't try to draw it accurately. Just scribble it down as fast as you can. You're just checking you know roughly where the battles were.

The Clash of Cultures

The advance of the settlers made life harder for the <u>Native Americans</u>.

Many settlers viewed the Native Americans as Inferior

1) The <u>stereotypical</u> Native American in settlers' eyes was <u>lazy</u> and <u>savage</u>. Many settlers believed their own culture of <u>private property</u> and more <u>intensive land use</u> should have priority over tribal rights to the land.

2) <u>Exceptions</u> to this attitude tended to belong to those settlers like former mountain man Jim Bridger who <u>knew</u> the Native Americans best.

Population Pressures led to Conflict

1) In <u>1830</u>, the US government gave the whole of the <u>Great Plains</u> over to the <u>Native Americans</u>. The eastern edge of the Plains was known as the <u>permanent Indian frontier</u>.

2) At the time, most settlers viewed this land as wild and inhospitable. It was known as the "<u>Great American Desert</u>".

3) But the population of the US was rapidly increasing. In 1843 pioneers began the <u>great migration</u>, moving west <u>across the Plains</u> to Oregon and California in search of <u>land</u>.

4) This migration caused some disruption to the herds which the Native Americans hunted, but on the whole it meant <u>trade opportunities</u> for the Plains Indians.

5) The first major problems began with the <u>Gold Rush</u> in 1849. Hunting and gathering were so <u>disrupted</u> by the mines that many Plains Indians were left near <u>starvation</u>. Worse still were the <u>diseases</u> brought by the miners. Native American numbers in California dropped from <u>100 000</u> in 1846 to <u>30 000</u> in 1870.

6) Increasingly during the <u>1850s</u> and <u>1860s</u>, tribes <u>fought</u> the settlers and the US army.

Native Americans were forced onto Reservations

1) The US government often tried to <u>reserve</u> lands where tribes could be <u>confined</u> by <u>treaty</u>.

2) The problem tended to be that the lands, if <u>poor</u>, were <u>insufficient</u> for the tribes, and if <u>good</u>, were grabbed by <u>settlers</u> in defiance of the treaties. Likewise, many chiefs <u>lacked</u> the <u>authority</u> to compel their people's adherence to these agreements.

3) The example of the <u>South-West</u> shows how <u>outcomes varied</u>:

- The <u>Navajos</u> achieved <u>peace and prosperity</u> after <u>1868</u> when a <u>treaty</u> with the US allowed them sufficient reservation area in their homeland.
- The <u>Apaches</u> under Cochise and Geronimo <u>fought against</u> confinement until their surrender in 1886 because their <u>San Carlos reservation</u> was hot and malarial.

Outside the Reservations, there were often Problems

1) By the 1830s, the Cherokees in Georgia had taken to <u>settled farming</u> and lived in European-style <u>houses</u>. They also published a newspaper in their <u>own alphabet</u>.

2) President Jackson, under the <u>Indian Removal Act</u> of <u>1830</u>, authorised their <u>forced expulsion</u> from Georgia to what is now Oklahoma. This eventually happened in 1838, and 4000 Cherokees died on the way — an event they called the "<u>Trail of Tears</u>".

My tooth hurts — too many treaties...

More hard times for the Native Americans, I'm afraid. One thing it's worth remembering is the <u>huge growth</u> in the settler population — it's like the Native Americans just got <u>squeezed out</u>. But some tribes did better than others — make sure you know the reasons <u>why</u>.

War and Peace on the Plains

Neither <u>treaties</u> nor <u>wars</u> halted the settlement of the West.

The 1851 Fort Laramie Treaty bought a few years' peace

1) To protect the <u>Oregon Trail</u> the US government wanted to create a safe corridor across the plains.
2) A gathering of about 10 000 <u>Sioux</u>, <u>Shoshonis</u>, <u>Cheyennes</u>, <u>Crows</u> and <u>Arapahos</u> assembled in council near <u>Fort Laramie</u>, Wyoming.
3) The tribes granted <u>transit rights</u> across the plains and allowed the US to build <u>forts</u> along the trail.
4) Each tribe agreed to remain within its own <u>defined territory</u> — so each could be held responsible for attacks in that area. This was the first attempt at a <u>reservation</u> system on the Great Plains.
5) In return the US promised the signatories <u>annuities</u> (annual payments). These were later <u>reduced</u> by Congress.
6) In <u>1853</u> a similar treaty signed with the <u>Comanches</u> and <u>Kiowas</u> of the southern plains obtained protection for the <u>Santa Fe Trail</u>.
7) The treaties were <u>stopgaps</u> only. From <u>1855</u> various wars resumed between the US and northern plains tribes.

The Civil War (1861-5) was mainly fought in the East

1) Between <u>1861 and 1865</u> the US was torn by <u>civil war</u> — an unsuccessful bid for independence by a <u>Confederacy</u> of eleven Southern states who wanted to continue allowing <u>slavery</u>.
2) <u>Westward migration</u> of settlers continued during the war.
3) Most of the fighting was East of the Mississippi, but attempts were made by both sides to <u>involve</u> the Native Americans.
4) The war had a vital effect on the cattle trade. (See p.17.)
5) Many Civil War soldiers — including <u>Custer</u>, <u>Sherman</u> and <u>Sheridan</u> — went on to be involved in conflicts with the Plains Indians.

Little Crow's War was an uprising in Minnesota, 1862

1) The <u>Santee Sioux</u>, also known as the <u>Dakota</u>, had been peaceful, <u>accepting</u> reservation life and adopting the white settlers' ways. Their chief, Little Crow, wore a jacket and trousers, went to church and took up farming. But Civil War <u>shortages</u>, a delay in payment of their <u>annuity</u>, <u>cheating</u> by traders and a poor harvest left his people near <u>starvation</u>.
2) In August, four Dakota returning from an unsuccessful hunt <u>murdered</u> five settlers for a dare.
3) Fearing <u>retaliation</u> on the entire tribe, Little Crow reluctantly led his warriors in an uprising made easier by the <u>absence of many troops</u> away fighting the Civil War. Hundreds of settlers and about 100 soldiers were killed, and the town of <u>New Ulm</u> burned, before the Dakota were defeated at <u>Wood Lake</u> in September.
4) 38 Dakota prisoners were <u>hanged</u> in December, and most of the Dakota were <u>expelled</u> from what was left of their land.

The Indian Wars — hardly civil affairs...

The Indian Wars were a major episode in American West history — and generated much <u>controversy</u> and <u>bitterness</u> still felt today.

Early Conflicts on the Plains

Many Indians wanted peace, but in the end were <u>forced into conflict</u>.

The Cheyenne Uprising and Sand Creek — 1864

1) In <u>April 1864</u>, after a dispute over cattle, many Cheyenne began <u>raids</u> on ranches and stagecoaches, committing <u>atrocities</u> which outraged Denver <u>public opinion</u>.
2) In August the governor of Colorado Territory issued a <u>proclamation</u> urging the <u>hunting down</u> of "hostile Indians". Volunteers then shot at every Cheyenne they could find.
3) Chief <u>Black Kettle</u> wanted peace and a safe winter camp. <u>Army officers</u> promised him <u>protection</u> if he would move to <u>Sand Creek</u>.
4) On the <u>29th November 1864</u>, Colonel <u>John Chivington</u> attacked Black Kettle's camp with a force of 700 volunteers. Of the 500 in the camp, about 163 were <u>killed</u> — 110 of those were women and children. The rest, including Black Kettle, <u>escaped</u>.
5) The volunteers returned to Denver, <u>displaying scalps</u> as <u>trophies</u>. But some people were sickened, and the massacre was <u>investigated</u> by Congress. Chivington was <u>condemned</u>, but never punished.
6) Meanwhile the Cheyenne, Arapaho and Sioux <u>retaliated</u> by burning more ranches and stage stations. They too killed women and children. The central plains erupted into <u>war</u>.
7) In a further massacre at the <u>Washita River</u>, Oklahoma in 1868, Black Kettle — still hoping for peace — was killed by <u>Lt. Col. George Custer's</u> soldiers.

Red Cloud's War and the Bozeman Trail — 1866

1) The <u>Bozeman Trail</u> connected the Platte River with the <u>mines</u> in Montana. It passed through the <u>hunting grounds</u> of the Sioux, which had been guaranteed to them by the <u>Fort Laramie Treaty</u> of <u>1851</u>.
2) The army wanted to build <u>forts</u> on the trail to protect travellers from Indians. Talks were held with <u>Red Cloud</u> in <u>1866</u>, one of the Sioux leaders. The talks failed when the Sioux saw soldiers marching out to begin building <u>before any deal</u> had been struck.
3) <u>Col. H.B. Carrington</u> started building three forts. He was harassed by groups of Plains Indians, including <u>Sitting Bull</u> and <u>Crazy Horse</u>.

Red Cloud

4) Several skirmishes occurred outside the forts. In December 1866 <u>Capt. W.J. Fetterman's</u> force was ambushed and destroyed. Around 100 soldiers died.
5) Bad weather saved the rest of Carrington's force, but the army had to negotiate what was effectively a <u>surrender</u>. The Bozeman Trail <u>forts</u> were <u>abandoned</u>, and <u>burned</u> by the Native Americans.
6) Red Cloud then consented to the <u>Fort Laramie Treaty of 1868</u> — in which the US gave the Sioux western South Dakota as a <u>reservation</u> and agreed not to re-fortify the Bozeman Trail. Red Cloud <u>promised</u> never again to make war on the settlers — and kept his promise.

I bet Carrington had reservations after that...

The Indian Wars weren't just one war. They were a <u>series</u> of intermittent and localised conflicts, fought against different tribes — not against one united nation. Make sure you remember the <u>key people</u> involved — on both sides. Make a <u>list</u> of them, and make sure you can write a bit about <u>what each of them did</u>. Learn a few <u>dates</u> too — and impress those examiners.

Reservations and the Little Bighorn

The forcing of Native Americans into <u>smaller and smaller reservations</u> could not go on indefinitely.

The Railroad took Land from the Native Americans

1) <u>Violating treaties</u>, the <u>railroads</u> ran through Native American lands.
2) Vast numbers of <u>buffalo</u> were <u>slaughtered</u> to feed the construction gangs.
3) The tribes resisted bitterly, derailing trains and ambushing workmen. General <u>Sherman</u> built <u>forts</u> to safeguard the railroad.
4) Much more than a mere transport corridor across the Plains, the railroad was funded by <u>land grants</u> of ten square miles for every mile of track — land soon sold to settlers.

Think we went a bit overboard?

Can't be too careful though, can you?

The Sioux Campaign (1876) — Climax of the Indian Wars

1) In <u>1874</u> troops under <u>Lt. Col. George Custer</u> confirmed the presence of gold in the <u>Black Hills of Dakota</u>. The hills were sacred to the Sioux and had been guaranteed to them by the Fort Laramie Treaty of <u>1868</u>.
2) Despite <u>government opposition</u> a gold rush started, centering on the town of <u>Deadwood</u>.
3) <u>Sitting Bull</u> and <u>Crazy Horse</u> raised the largest Native American force ever seen (about <u>4000</u> warriors).
4) The Army sent to oppose this uprising was led by <u>Gen. George Crook</u>. Crook hoped to <u>split</u> the Indian force, but ended up splitting his own instead. This error was made worse by the ambitious <u>Custer</u>, who deliberately sought the chance to attack the Native Americans alone.
5) Custer was outnumbered more than <u>5 to 1</u> as he entered the valley of the <u>Little Bighorn</u>. He didn't even have the advantage of <u>technology</u> — many of the Indians were armed with repeating <u>Winchester</u> rifles, while Custer's soldiers had single-shot <u>Springfields</u>.
6) Custer and all 225 of his command were killed. This was the <u>greatest</u> Native American <u>victory</u> in battle against the US army.
7) Yet it came <u>too late</u>. Wiping out Custer's command could not bring back the buffalo, end the Black Hills gold rush or stop the tide of settlement.

Lt. Col. George Custer

- In <u>1876</u>, the US army launched a <u>winter campaign</u> in which the Sioux were beaten by <u>hunger</u> and the loss of their <u>horses</u>. <u>Sitting Bull</u> retreated to <u>Canada</u>.
- Crazy Horse surrendered in <u>May 1877</u> to the Agency (reservation) of Red Cloud. He was later <u>killed</u> by some of his own people while resisting arrest.

I don't get it — was it a little or a big horn?...

Custer's defeat at the Battle of Little Bighorn is one of the most <u>famous events</u> in Western History. Custer became a hero for many Americans — but even at the time there were those who criticised him. But in the end it was a <u>small victory</u> for the Native Americans in a war they couldn't win.

Prophets of White Destruction

A string of Native American <u>prophets</u> emerged to tell of glorious changes of fortune.

Chato and Geronimo led a campaign from Mexico

Geronimo

1) In <u>1881</u> a medicine man (see p.7) called <u>Nakaidoklini</u> said his medicine could raise dead warriors and clear the settlers from Arizona.
2) This led to a revolt by reservation <u>Apaches</u> and a mutiny by Apache <u>army scouts</u> on <u>30th August 1881</u>. There followed a very cruel cross-border campaign led by <u>Chato</u> and the non-chief Goyathlay, better known as <u>Geronimo</u>. It was only defeated by <u>cooperation</u> between the US and Mexican governments in <u>1883</u> and <u>1884</u>. The main army officers involved were Generals Crook and Miles.
3) Several more outbreaks of Native American violence occurred, some fuelled by <u>alcohol</u>. Geronimo surrendered for the final time on <u>4th Sept. 1886</u>.

Ghost Dancers and Wounded Knee — 29th Dec. 1890

1) The seer <u>Wovoka</u> taught that a special <u>Ghost Dance</u> could raise the dead and bring a new world free from the settlers. He was opposed to violence, but his teachings were taken as a <u>call for war</u>.
2) Some Sioux followers of the movement believed that special <u>shirts</u> would <u>protect them</u> from the bullets of the Americans.
3) <u>Sitting Bull</u> had retreated into Canada after the <u>1876</u> campaign. He joined Buffalo Bill's Wild West Show in <u>1885</u>, but soon returned to the reservation. He was killed in a bungled attempt to <u>arrest</u> him on <u>15th Dec. 1890</u>. The government wrongly thought he was a leader of the Ghost Dance movement.
4) At roughly the same time <u>Big Foot</u> of the Sioux was camped at <u>Wounded Knee</u> to avoid the trouble that was brewing.

Sitting Bull

5) Troops caught up with him and tried to <u>disarm the Sioux</u>. One warrior fired a shot. The troops replied with a volley, killing 52. Survivors went on to fight by hand.
6) The battle <u>escalated</u> when <u>more warriors</u> from the Agency camp nearby heard the gunfire and swarmed out, shooting at the soldiers, then disappearing into the prairie.

- The <u>Battle of Wounded Knee</u> cost the lives of some 150 Sioux — about 60 of them women and children — and 25 soldiers.
- It marked the <u>final suppression</u> of Native Americans by armed <u>force</u>. By mid-January 1891 the dispersed warriors had all <u>surrendered</u>.
- The sight of ghost-dance <u>shirts</u> pierced by <u>bullets</u> destroyed the tribes' faith in a magical restoration of the old way of life. The <u>reservation</u> was reluctantly accepted as <u>home</u>.

A terrible end to the Native American fight for freedom...

The Wounded Knee massacre was the <u>last</u> major "battle" of the Indian Wars — the US <u>government</u> had won. Think about the reasons for their victory — and the role played by each of the following on each side: <u>deception</u>, <u>mistrust</u>, <u>revenge</u>, <u>emotion</u> and <u>bad discipline</u>.

The End of the Frontier

America's population was growing — increasing the pressure on reservation land.

Native Americans were Pressured to drop their Culture

1) The formerly-nomadic Plains Indians, now confined to smaller areas, could no longer feed or clothe themselves without government aid.
2) Many millions of buffalo had been slaughtered by the white settlers for their hides. The great reduction in buffalo numbers had a big impact on the Native Americans, particularly those Plains Indian tribes whose way of life had been focused on hunting buffalo (see p.5).
3) Living on hand-outs, they became demoralised and there were high rates of alcoholism.
4) Their dependency put them under the control of government officials who tried to suppress their cultural identity. Many children were taken away to be educated, for example at the Carlisle Indian School in Pennsylvania. Plural marriages, and religious practices such as the Sun Dance, were banned. The threat of withholding rations was used to enforce cooperation.

Americans became aware of the End of the Frontier

1) In 1890, census results revealed that — unlike in 1880 — there was no longer a definable Western frontier of settlement. The frontier was declared officially closed.
2) This didn't mean that there was no more land available for settlers, but what remained was in isolated pockets and the best areas had been taken.
3) Land-hungry white Americans now wanted steps taken to carve up the reservations.

The Dawes Act (1887) Parcelled Out tribal lands

1) The aim of the Dawes Act was to convert tribesmen into independent farmers.
2) The Act allowed reservations to be broken up into allotments — these were given out to individual tribe members to own and farm.
3) This idea went against Native American tradition — land was usually shared by the tribe.
4) Under the Act, each head of family was assigned 160 acres, each single adult 80 acres and each minor 40 acres. US citizenship was also part of the deal.
5) The Act had been called for by reformers who believed that reservation life encouraged idleness, and others who just wanted to get their hands on more land.
6) When all the inhabitants of a reservation had been assigned their holdings, the remaining surplus land was thrown open to white settlement.
7) In 1934, the government reversed its policy, repealing the Dawes Act and encouraging tribal identities. But by that time, Native Americans had lost over 60 per cent of their original reservation lands.
8) Lands belonging to five tribes (Cherokee, Chickasaw, Choctaw, Creek and Seminole) were exempt from the Dawes Act, yet through forced sales they too were eventually handed over. In the Oklahoma Land Rush of 22 April 1889, 15 000 settlers raced across the starting line to seize what had been the Cherokee Strip.

The frontier closed — and the West is history...

Here endeth the American West — the US extending from sea to shining sea, and the Native Americans squeezed onto an ever smaller share of the land. Make sure you know the narrative of how things ended up this way — it's all very well knowing all the little facts, but you've got to know how they all fit together.

Revision Summary for Sections 5-6

The last page of Western questions. Don't forget to go through these regularly — and make sure you can do them all. And if you can do these, get hold of some of those ghastly exam questions. After all, they're the ones that count. You know it makes sense...

1) What is meant by a "federal system of government"?

2) How big did the population of a territory need to be for it to become a state?

3) What three products were the main sources of revenue in America?

4) What became known as the "Western Civil War of Incorporation"?

5) How did the James Younger gang gain their 'Robin Hood' reputation? Who was their leader?

6) What became known as the "range wars"? Give an example of this type of conflict.

7) Who was Wyatt Earp? What did he get up to?

8) What are "vigilante groups"?

9) Describe the events leading up to the Johnson County War in 1892.

10) What was the attitude of many settlers towards the Native Americans?

11) What was the 'permanent Indian frontier'?

12) How did many early settlers view the Great Plains?

13) Why did Indian numbers in California drop from 100 000 in 1846 to 30 000 in 1870?

14) What were the reservations?

15) How did the experiences of the Navajo and Apache tribes vary with respect to the reservations?

16) How had the Cherokees tried to fit into European ways in Georgia and Texas, and how were they repaid?

17) What was agreed at the 1851 Fort Laramie Treaty?

18) Name three cavalry commanders who learnt their trade in the Civil War.

19) Describe the events that led to Little Crow's war in 1862. What was the outcome?

20) Describe the events at Sand Creek on the 29th of November 1864 and what led to them.

21) Why was the Bozeman Trail important to: a) the Sioux Indians? b) the settlers?

22) What did the 1868 Fort Laramie Treaty offer the Sioux people?

23) Discuss the reasons behind the Sioux Campaign of 1876.

24) a) Who commanded the army forces in the Sioux campaign of 1876?
    b) Who led the Native American forces?

25) What happened at the Little Bighorn?

26) What did the Native Americans believe performing the Ghost Dance would achieve?

27) What happened at Wounded Knee in December 1890?

28) How did the US government attempt to suppress the cultural identities of the Plains Indians?

29) In what year was the Western frontier officially declared closed?

30) Describe the 1887 Dawes Act and what it set out to achieve.

Important Dates

Here's a <u>timeline</u> showing the <u>order</u> of important events in the history of medicine.

Critical events and Turning points

BC

c.3000 — Writing developing in Egypt

c.400 — Cult of Asclepios popular

c. 420-350 — Hippocratic Corpus

0

129 — Birth of Galen

476 — Fall of Rome

663 — Synod of Whitby

980-1037 — Life of Avicenna

1348 — Black Death

1454 — Printing in Europe

1660 — Founding of Royal Society

1665 — Great Plague of London

1720 — Inoculation in Britain

1796 — First vaccination

1831 — Cholera in Britain

1842 — Chadwick Report

1846/7 — Ether and Chloroform in use

1848 — 1st Public Health Act

1854 — Cholera linked to water pollution (Snow)

1857 — Germ Theory (Pasteur)

1875 — Public Health Act

1890 — Antiseptic in general use

1895 — First X-rays

1896 — Becquerel discovers radioactivity

1900 — Blood groups discovered

1906 — Liberal Reforms

1928 — Penicillin (Fleming)

1939 - 45 — World War II

1951 — First kidney transplant

1953 — Structure of DNA identified

Late 1950s — The Pill

1981 — AIDS discovered

AD

Egyptian culture

Greek culture

Roman Empire

Islamic Empire

Important People

The history of medicine has some real <u>heroes</u> — learn who they were and when they were about.

Learn about the most Important People

<u>Thousands</u> and thousands of people have <u>contributed</u> to the development of medicine. We've mentioned quite a few in this book — but some were <u>more influential</u> than others. Here are the <u>dates</u> of some of the important ones. You should be able to say what contribution each of them made to medicine. For many you should know enough to be able to write a <u>short essay</u> on their work and contribution — and you could be asked to in the exam.

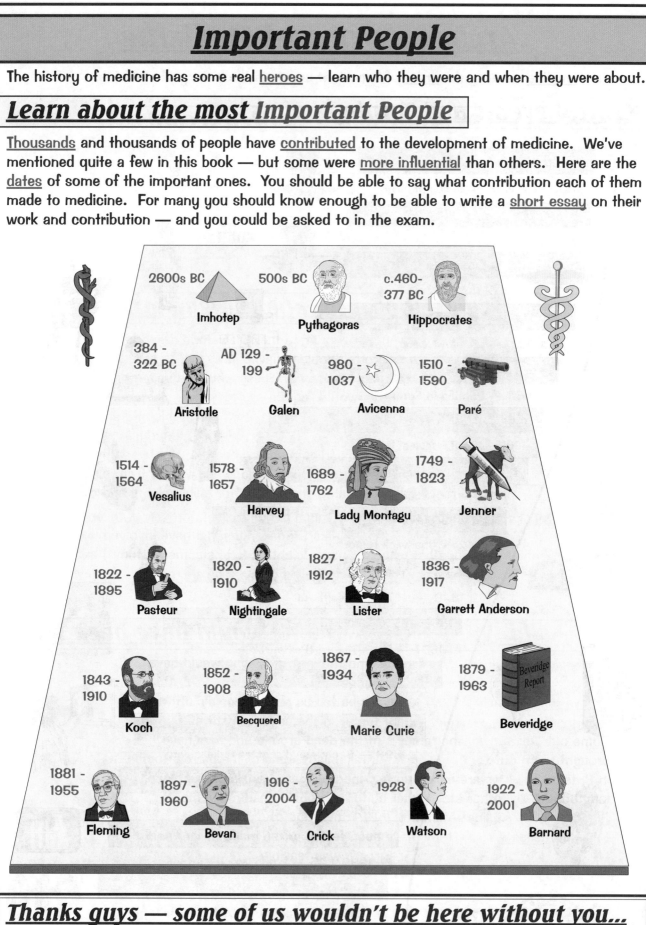

2600s BC — Imhotep	500s BC — Pythagoras	c.460-377 BC — Hippocrates
384 - 322 BC — Aristotle	AD 129 - 199 — Galen	980 - 1037 — Avicenna / 1510 - 1590 — Paré
1514 - 1564 — Vesalius	1578 - 1657 — Harvey	1689 - 1762 — Lady Montagu / 1749 - 1823 — Jenner
1822 - 1895 — Pasteur	1820 - 1910 — Nightingale	1827 - 1912 — Lister / 1836 - 1917 — Garrett Anderson
1843 - 1910 — Koch	1852 - 1908 — Becquerel	1867 - 1934 — Marie Curie / 1879 - 1963 — Beveridge
1881 - 1955 — Fleming	1897 - 1960 — Bevan	1916 - 2004 — Crick / 1928 - — Watson / 1922 - 2001 — Barnard

Thanks guys — some of us wouldn't be here without you...

Without these people life would be a lot less pleasant than it is. So I guess we all owe them a debt of <u>gratitude</u> — one that you can start repaying by learning about their work. These timelines should help you keep all your history of medicine facts in the <u>right order</u> — so it's worth your while having a look at it every now and then as you work your way through the topic.

Archaeology and Medicine

OK, time to get down to the details. <u>Prehistory</u> is when it all started.

Prehistory _is the time Before_ written records

<u>Prehistory</u> is defined as the time <u>before written records</u>, which means that it ended at different times for different societies. Some societies are <u>still</u> in prehistory, as they don't yet have <u>writing</u>. Writing was introduced to Britain by the <u>Romans</u>, who conquered in 43 AD.

Although we can never be totally sure what life was like in <u>prehistory</u> (or history for that matter), combining different sorts of <u>evidence</u> can allow us to make a good guess.

<u>Archaeology</u> can tell us a lot about prehistoric people

Stonehenge

1) <u>Cave paintings</u> and other prehistoric artwork indicate that prehistoric people believed in a <u>spiritual world</u>. It's likely that their <u>explanations</u> of illness would be based on <u>evil spirits</u>, and illnesses would require <u>spiritual or religious</u> cures.

2) Archaeology also tells us that our prehistoric ancestors were mostly <u>nomadic hunter-gatherers</u>, although <u>agriculture</u> developed before the earliest written records. Hunter-gatherers lived in <u>small extended family</u> groups and moved from place to place following game and looking for edible plants and other resources.

3) <u>Social organisation</u> probably didn't extend much beyond <u>family structures</u>, even after the invention of agriculture. <u>Special projects</u> like Stonehenge must have involved large numbers. These probably came together when <u>food</u> was plentiful (late summer/autumn) and then split up in winter. Such gatherings would have allowed ideas to be <u>shared</u>.

Progress _in Prehistoric Medicine_ would have been slow

1) The infrequency of mass gatherings and the <u>lack of writing</u> would have made any progress in medical knowledge <u>slow</u>.

2) <u>Excavations</u> of ancient burials and tombs tell us about people's attitudes to <u>human remains</u> — an important factor in the advancement of <u>anatomy</u>. Some cultures <u>moved</u> the remains of the dead around and may have brought them out for <u>ceremonial purposes</u>. In some of the barrow tombs in Britain skeletons are mixed up and incomplete — skulls in one place, long bones in another etc. Other cultures probably had many more <u>taboos</u> about remains — limiting their knowledge of <u>anatomy</u>.

3) Fine and <u>delicate</u> stone tools have been found, often made of flint and obsidian, which show that some <u>surgery</u> was feasible.

<u>Before writing there were no revision guides...</u>

The key point about prehistory is of course that there's no writing. There's nothing to tell us what they believed — so we have to <u>deduce</u> things. Different prehistoric societies would have had different ideas about things. Bear in mind there's been a lot more human prehistory (<u>hundreds of thousands of years</u>) than there has been history (a few thousand years).

Ancient Health and Beliefs

We don't just have to rely on <u>archaeology</u> though — we can look at <u>other societies</u> too.

Aboriginal Cultures give us clues about prehistory

<u>Outsiders</u> visiting prehistoric societies can produce <u>written records</u> of what they see — but their very contact can often <u>change</u> the society they look at.

1) Ancient artefacts and artwork are sometimes <u>similar</u> to things made by modern or more recent <u>aboriginal</u> societies in Australia and elsewhere. <u>Attitudes and practices</u> of modern aborigines have therefore been used in <u>guessing</u> what ancient people thought and did.

2) Some modern aboriginal medicine combines basic practical methods like <u>setting broken bones</u> and bandaging with <u>spiritual explanations</u> of illness and cure.

3) Witch doctors, shamans and 'medicine men' are frequently credited with the ability to both <u>cure and inflict</u> illness.

4) <u>Preventative</u> medicine (warding off evil) is practised as well as <u>healing</u> (driving off evil). <u>Rituals</u> and <u>sacrifice</u> are often involved. Rituals might involve the use of herbs, potions and techniques of practical value — but they are seen as <u>magic</u> rather than medicine.

Archaeopathology is the study of ancient disease

1) <u>Archaeopathology</u> is the study of <u>ancient bodies</u> to see what <u>diseases</u> and <u>health problems</u> they had, how they were treated, and how the people <u>died</u>.

2) Most <u>prehistoric</u> bodies have decayed to <u>just bones</u> or even <u>further</u>. This limits the <u>evidence</u> that can be gained from them — e.g. you couldn't tell if someone died from a heart attack, or if they'd had surgery on soft tissues.

3) Some bodies, preserved in <u>ice</u>, <u>peat bogs</u> or by <u>mummification</u>, still have <u>soft tissues</u> remaining. They're very important for what they tell us about prehistoric <u>health and medicine</u>.

4) <u>Trephining</u> or <u>trepanning</u> is the cutting of <u>holes</u> in people's heads. Some skulls show that <u>people survived</u> the operation because the bone continued to grow afterwards. We cannot be certain <u>why</u> people did this but it may have been to allow <u>evil spirits</u> out or to grant special powers of <u>communication</u> with the spirit world.

Of course it works! No-one ever complains of a headache twice!

5) There is <u>modern evidence</u> that trephining can lead to altered mental <u>sensations</u>. It is sometimes done by doctors when <u>head injuries</u> lead to a build-up of pressure inside the skull. So ancient trephining could have been done for <u>practical reasons</u> — to treat injury or in an attempt to treat diseases like epilepsy.

Trepanning — a hole load of fun...

Prehistoric societies would have had both a <u>practical</u> and a <u>spiritual</u> view of the world. Assumptions of <u>supernatural</u> causes for unexplained events would have <u>discouraged</u> investigation or experimentation — so medical development may have been r e a l s l o w.

The Ancient Egyptian Civilisation

The <u>Egyptians</u> were one of the most important civilisations in the ancient world.

The society of Ancient Egypt relied on the River Nile

1) The <u>Egyptian civilisation</u> was an <u>agricultural</u> one that spread in a narrow band along the river <u>Nile</u>. It thrived between <u>c.3400 BC</u> and <u>30 BC</u>. Every year the <u>Nile floods</u> fertilised the fields and the river provided <u>water for irrigation</u>.
2) The successful agriculture provided <u>spare food</u> so that more people could be <u>doctors</u>, <u>priests</u> (these two professions overlapped or were the same thing) and other <u>professionals</u>.
3) <u>Barges</u> on the Nile enabled fairly swift <u>transportation</u> and <u>communication</u> making trade and government easier.
4) The ancient Egyptians had <u>writing</u> — so <u>ideas</u> could be <u>recorded</u> and <u>communicated</u> better than in prehistoric societies.

The world of the Egyptians was controlled by the Gods

1) The <u>Egyptians</u> had a huge number of <u>gods</u> that controlled all aspects of life, including <u>illness</u> and <u>medicine</u>. <u>Amulets</u>, <u>charms</u> and <u>rituals</u> were used to avoid and cure illness.
2) <u>Sekhmet</u> was the <u>goddess of war</u>, who also sent and cured <u>epidemics</u>. <u>Thoth</u> was the god who gave doctors their ability to <u>cure people</u>. <u>Imhotep</u>, who was the <u>Pharaoh Zoser's</u> doctor in about <u>2630 BC</u>, was adopted as a <u>god of healing</u>. Doctors were <u>respected</u> people.
3) Priests kept the <u>Books of Thoth</u>, which contained the accepted <u>treatments and spells</u>. The books themselves have not survived but the <u>Papyrus Ebers</u> (so called because it was once owned by a German Egyptologist called Maurice Ebers) contains spells, potions (medicines) and procedures probably <u>taken</u> from the Books of Thoth.
4) Some of the <u>drugs</u> used by the Egyptians, including <u>opium</u>, are still used <u>today</u>. They were probably thought of as driving away <u>evil spirits</u> rather than affecting the way the <u>body works</u>.
5) The instructions are very <u>exact</u> as to what should be done, what medicines given and what words should be used in incantation and when talking to the patient.

The Egyptians actually Looked at their patients

1) <u>Diagnosis</u> means the <u>observation</u> of a patient and the <u>recognition</u> of their <u>symptoms</u>.
2) Even though it is simple in theory, diagnosis can be the most <u>important</u> part of the work of a doctor and can be quite <u>tricky</u>.
3) <u>Egyptian writings</u> survive that demonstrate that they included <u>diagnosis</u> in their <u>medical rituals</u>.

Nile desperandum — but there's a pharaohed bit to learn...

Don't ignore all those <u>background</u> details at the top of the page — info like that helps to put it all in perspective. You need to know the <u>factors</u> that influenced medicine in Egypt — so that stuff's essential. The most important point here is that the Egyptians believed diseases were caused by the <u>gods</u> — which of course had a big say in how they were <u>treated</u>.

Practical Medicine in Ancient Egypt

The Egyptians' understanding of the body was both helped and hindered by mummification.

The Egyptians Mummified dead bodies

1) The Egyptians believed that the human body would be needed by a person in the afterlife, and that material possessions would also be important. This led to them preserving bodies and entombing them with fabulous grave goods.
2) They prepared bodies for mummification by extracting soft organs such as the brain and the intestines, then drying (desiccating) what remained with salt. This gave the Egyptians some knowledge of anatomy.
3) They believed that destroying someone's body meant they wouldn't go to the afterlife, so experimental dissection was out. This limited the amount of knowledge that could be gained.
4) An Egyptian papyrus written around 1600 BC outlines some simple surgical procedures.
5) Carvings in the temple of Kom Ombo (c. 100 BC) show a variety of surgical instruments.
6) Willow was used after surgery and to treat wounds. It contains salicylic acid, a mild antiseptic and the original source of aspirin.

Non-spiritual causes for illness were suggested

1) The River Nile led some Egyptians to suggest that, like the Nile delta or their irrigation systems, the body was full of channels.
2) They thought that if those channels were blocked this led to disease. This led them to use vomiting, purging (laxatives) and bleeding to clear the various passages. Such treatments may have helped with some complaints.
3) Such ideas were not accepted by everyone and the people who believed them did not abandon spiritual explanations and treatments.
4) The Egyptians knew diet was important — medical procedures included recommended foods.

The Egyptians kept themselves Clean

1) The Egyptians valued cleanliness. They bathed, shaved their heads and had toilets. They also changed their clothes regularly.
2) In the Egyptian climate this would have made life more comfortable, but hygiene also appears to have had a religious significance. Priests washed more often than others and would shave their whole bodies before important ceremonies.
3) Egyptian toilets have been found, but they did not have water-fed sewers so the toilets had to be emptied manually.
4) Egyptians also developed mosquito nets which would have offered some protection from malaria.

Mummification — the onset of parenthood...

One of the reasons we know so much about Ancient Egyptian medicine is because they wrote things down. Ancient Egyptian writing was done in little pictures called hieroglyphics. It allowed for their ideas about the human body and its diseases to pass down the generations. Writing is hugely important for medicine — having access to different texts is a key theme.

The Ancient Greek Civilisation

All around the Mediterranean the Greeks developed a <u>supernatural approach</u> to medicine.

Greek Culture spread across southern Europe...

1) The notion of countries bounded by <u>geographical borders</u> — lines on a map — is rather recent. When we talk of the <u>ancient Greeks</u> we are referring not to people who lived in Greece, but to people who lived the way the Greeks did — they were <u>culturally Greek</u>.
2) Greek civilisation was made up of independent <u>city states</u> around the shores of the Mediterranean and the Black Sea.
3) Greek culture flourished between around <u>700 BC</u> and <u>300 BC</u> and its medicine was <u>influenced</u> by the Egyptians.
4) They believed the world was controlled by <u>many gods</u>, and they told and wrote down heroic tales (myths) about people, gods and monsters. They also loved to <u>debate</u>.

Greek culture involved lots of <u>debate</u>. Loads of views were expressed, but being in the more fierce debates could be <u>dangerous</u>. The philosopher Socrates' <u>enemies</u> charged him with impiety and corrupting the young — and sentenced him to death. Two systems of medicine flourished side by side: one based on <u>religion</u> and one on <u>logical philosophy</u>.

Asclepios was the Greek god of healing

1) A <u>spiritual/supernatural</u> approach to medicine was followed by the cult of <u>Asclepios</u>, god of healing. His temples were called <u>Asclepions</u> and people went to stay at them when they were ill — much like we might visit a <u>health farm</u>, or like Catholics might go on a pilgrimage to <u>Lourdes</u>. The cult was most popular in the <u>5th</u> and <u>4th centuries BC</u>.
2) Visitors were expected to undergo <u>ceremonial washing</u> in the sea, make a <u>sacrifice</u> to the god and sleep in a building called an <u>abaton</u>. An abaton was a narrow building with a roof but no solid walls so that it was <u>open to the air</u>. Whilst sleeping there the god was supposed to come to them in a <u>dream</u> and <u>cure</u> them.

I feel better already, thanks.

3) Priests also did "ward rounds", administering <u>ointments</u> and performing <u>rituals</u>, some of which involved placing <u>snakes</u> on the patients. The snake is the sacred animal of Asclepios and can still be seen in the <u>logos</u> of many medical organisations.
4) Success stories were recorded in <u>inscriptions</u> on the walls of the Asclepions.
5) Asclepios's daughters, <u>Hygeia and Panacea</u>, were also involved in healing. Their names developed into words used in modern medicine (hygiene — cleanliness, and panacea — a remedy for all ills). <u>Women</u> were allowed to be doctors in Ancient Greece.

Medicine in Grease? I bet they were smooth operators...

The key points here are that Greece was a <u>culture</u> rather than a country, and the Greeks believed in <u>many gods</u> — hence their belief in supernatural causes and cures. Remember that it's not enough to just learn these facts by rote — you've got to be prepared for the sort of things they'll ask you in the exam. It'd really help if you could work through some <u>past papers</u>.

Practical Medicine in Ancient Greece

Not all Greeks left it to the gods though — they also developed a "natural" approach to medicine.

Philosophers tried to explain things Rationally

1) Greek philosophers sought to devise rational explanations and logical codes of conduct. They attracted bands of followers such as the brotherhood of Pythagoras. These followers became devotees and argued with other philosophers. Religion was interwoven with their logic.

2) Thales of Miletus, founder of Greek philosophy, thought that water was the basis of life (c.580 BC). Anaximander (c.560 BC) said all things were made of four elements: earth, air, water and fire. Pythagoras (c.580-c.500 BC) thought life was about the balance of opposites.

Hippocrates — the Founding Father of Western medicine

1) Hippocrates (c.460-c.377BC) is acknowledged as the founding father of modern medicine. He was born on the island of Kos, travelled a bit and then taught medicine in Kos before dying in Larissa. Very little else is known about him but he is associated with the Hippocratic Oath and the Hippocratic Corpus.

2) The Hippocratic Oath is a promise made by doctors to obey rules of behaviour in their professional lives. Medical ethics are based on the Hippocratic Oath.

3) The Hippocratic Corpus is a collection of medical books, some of which might have been written by Hippocrates or his followers. It is probably what survived of the library of the Kos school of medicine at which Hippocrates taught.

> At last! A clear diagnosis — you're dead!

The ideas of the Hippocratic Corpus

1) Hippocrates saw the healthy body as being in balance — he thought that illness was an imbalance of the elements.

2) 'Airs, Waters and Places' a book from the Hippocratic Corpus looks for environmental causes for disease — not gods or spirits.

3) The books 'Prognostic', 'Coan Prognostic' and 'Aphorisms' improved on the Egyptian ideas of diagnosis. They suggest that, by studying enough cases, a doctor could learn to predict the course of an illness.

4) They also encourage the use of the four-step method for treating illness that we would now call the "clinical method of observation".

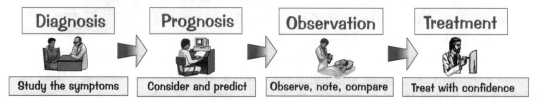

Diagnosis	Prognosis	Observation	Treatment
Study the symptoms	Consider and predict	Observe, note, compare	Treat with confidence

5) They suggest that no action should be taken before a reliable diagnosis is made. Illnesses should also, where possible, be left to run their course. Today we call this "Minimum Intervention".

Hippocrates — hard to spell? Think Hippo Crates

Make sure you see how Hippocrates' ideas fitted in with other Greek thought at the time. Remember that for hundreds of years his natural approach existed side by side with the supernatural ideas of the cult of Asclepios.

Practical Medicine in Ancient Greece

The Ancient Greeks were big believers in healthy living.

The Ancient Greeks had Lifestyle Regimens

1) 'A Regimen for Health' and 'Regimen in Acute Diseases', both from the Hippocratic Corpus, recommended lifestyles for healthy living or recovery from illness.
2) The Ancient Greeks believed that to be healthy they needed to exercise. Men and boys spent a lot of time in the gymnasium — a public area in part devoted to sport and physical training.
3) Hygiene was important, with emphasis placed on washing — keeping skin, hair and teeth clean.
4) While most Greek cities would have had little public sanitation, ancient Athens had a system which brought in clean water using clay pipes.
5) Diet was also thought to be important. 'A Regimen for Health' suggested a diet which changed with the seasons — eating as much as possible in winter, but drinking little — while in the summer drinking more and eating less.
6) This text also prescribes the amount of sleep and exercise required by people, depending on whether they have digestive problems.

Aristotle linked disease to the Four Humours

1) Aristotle (384-322 BC) developed the Hippocratic balance of elements to suggest that the body was made up of four fluids or humours — blood, phlegm, yellow bile and black bile. These were linked to the four seasons and the four elements. They needed to be in balance for good health.

2) In winter we get colds and produce more phlegm. Also, it rains more. This is why Aristotle linked water, winter and phlegm. Unfortunately, Aristotle failed to see that a bunged up nose, fevers and suchlike are symptoms or effects of disease. He thought they were the causes.

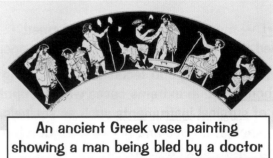

An ancient Greek vase painting showing a man being bled by a doctor

3) Treatments developed from the theory of the humours aimed at bringing the four back into balance. Some focused on getting rid of an excess of one or another of the humours (e.g. by getting rid of excess blood with bloodletting, or by giving an emetic — a substance that triggers vomiting) to rid the body of too much bile.

4) Other treatments aimed at counterbalancing the problem. Different foods, drinks, herbs and spices were considered as having a humour. Someone with a cold (too much cold, wet phlegm) could be given chicken, pepper or wine — all considered hot and dry — to correct the imbalance in the humours.

'Bile be black' — isn't that what Arnie said...

Just as Hippocrates had built on earlier ideas, so Aristotle built on Hippocrates' ideas. You could be asked about the development of medical ideas, so you need to think about things like that. The four humours were a big theory in medicine for a long time, and they continue to pop up right through the Middle Ages and beyond.

Medicine in Alexandria

With a lot of <u>books</u> and a little <u>dissection</u>, Alexandria put itself at the forefront of medicine.

Alexandria *became a centre of Medical Advance*

1) <u>Alexander the Great</u> (who was tutored by <u>Aristotle</u>) founded <u>Alexandria</u> in Egypt in <u>331 BC</u> as his new capital city. The <u>library</u> of Alexandria attempted to amass all the <u>knowledge</u> of the world. It made <u>copies</u> of books for other libraries, which was lucky as several <u>fires</u> eventually destroyed the collection.

2) Unlike in the rest of "Greece", <u>human dissection</u> was allowed in Alexandria. For a short time they even allowed <u>vivisection</u> (dissection when still alive) of condemned <u>criminals</u>. People began to see the human body as having served its purpose once the <u>soul</u> had left it.

3) Alexandria became famous for <u>training</u> medics and surgeons. Accurate <u>observation</u> was the key to much of the advancement made there. <u>Herophilus (c.335-280 BC)</u> compared human and animal anatomy and worked on the <u>nervous system</u>. He correctly identified the connections to the brain but thought the nerves were vessels carrying <u>pneuma</u> or life-force.

4) <u>Erasistratus (c.250 BC)</u> identified the differences between <u>arteries</u>, <u>veins</u> and <u>nerves</u> and saw that nerves were not hollow and so couldn't be vessels for fluid.

5) <u>Doctors</u> from Alexandria went to practise all over the world but also <u>divided</u> into competing intellectual camps which, whilst encouraging debate, also led doctors to refuse to consider anything except the teachings of their <u>own group</u>.

Surgery was a *Last Resort for the Ancient Greeks*

1) The mechanics of <u>surgery</u> advanced (which bits to cut, how to make the cut), but effective <u>anaesthetics</u>, <u>antiseptics</u> and the understanding of <u>germs</u> and infection were far in the future.

2) As a result surgery was a <u>risky procedure</u> with the patient often dying from trauma or infections such as sepsis.

3) Ancient Greeks only used surgery as a <u>last resort</u> — most treatments were performed outside the body. Exceptions to this rule included the draining of lungs infected with pneumonia.

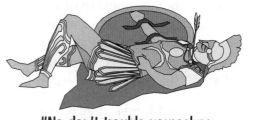

"No don't trouble yourselves. I'll walk it off."

4) Surgeons developed good techniques for setting <u>broken bones</u> and in extreme cases would amputate.

5) A range of <u>surgical instruments</u> such as scalpels, forceps, shears, probes and hooks were developed, made from iron, steel and brass.

6) Some Ancient Greek texts describe <u>eye operations</u> being carried out, possibly to remove cataracts and other foreign bodies.

Alexandria — great for medicine, not for human rights...

Alexandria was really important in the history of medicine because it allowed human <u>dissections</u> — a chance to have a good root around and see what things look like.
The massive <u>library</u> would've helped as well — loads of medical theories and observations brought together. I'm sure the human <u>vivisection</u> was helpful too, but I think I prefer libraries.

Civilisation and Public Health

Greek medicine didn't disappear with the decline of Greece — it lived on in the Roman Empire.

It took a while for the Romans to accept Greek Medicine

1) The Romans initially rejected the ideas of Greek medicine, which were still practised by Greeks around the Mediterranean.
2) As the Greek cities fell to the Romans in the 3rd and 2nd centuries BC many Greek doctors became slaves, and some were brought to Rome. But some Romans were suspicious of their ideas.
3) A plague in 293 BC led the Romans to establish an Asclepion in Rome, for which they brought a sacred snake from Epidaurus. This Asclepion survived throughout the Roman period and became a public hospital offering treatment to the poor and slaves.
4) Medicine and its mainly Greek practitioners slowly improved in status until Julius Caesar allowed doctors to become Roman citizens in 46 BC.

The Romans realised they needed a Healthy Army

1) The Romans were a very practical people. They realised that to build an empire you need a strong and healthy army.
2) The state paid for public doctors and hospitals for wounded soldiers called "valetudinaria".
3) The Roman Army had doctors in its ranks who were expected to carry out operations such as removing arrows from soldiers who had been hit.
4) Roman surgery became more advanced. Roman texts describe operations to remove bladder stones and cataracts that modern doctors believe would have been effective. Roman doctors had an increasingly sophisticated set of instruments.
5) Galen, a Greek doctor working in Rome (see next page), famously removed the infected breastbone from a patient. In his writings he listed a wide variety of eye operations he expected a good doctor to be able to carry out.

They took a Preventative Approach to Public Health

1) The Romans noticed that exposure to bad smells, unclean drinking water, sewage, swamps and dirt made you more likely to get ill.
2) They built aqueducts to carry clean water into cities. They also built public baths, toilets and sewers to remove waste. They drained swamps which were near towns.
3) Roman-style buildings and ideas about public health spread around their huge empire, which included much of Britain. For example, Chesters Fort on Hadrian's Wall contains a well-preserved Roman bath house.

Public Health — right up the Romans' street...

Just as the Egyptian culture didn't disappear as soon as the Greeks became more important, the Greeks didn't vanish when the Romans became the dominant culture. Think about how the two overlapping cultures led to continuity in medicine, and how the changes led to development. But just make sure you realise how important the Roman government was — what they did and why.

Dioscorides and Galen

Galen's work was influential for well over a thousand years — despite numerous inaccuracies.

Dioscorides wrote without mention of Superstitions

Dioscorides was a Greek doctor, born in Turkey, working for the Roman army in the 1st century AD. His book 'De Materia Medica' was the first on plants as medicines without lots of superstition.

Galen left an enduring legacy — despite many Mistakes

1) Galen was a Greek born in Pergamum (a Greek city in western Turkey) in AD 129. Pergamum had become part of the Roman empire in 133 BC.
2) Pergamum had an important Asclepion at which Galen first began his training before going to Smyrna and Alexandria.
3) He returned to Pergamum where he was doctor to the gladiators and then went to Rome in AD 161.
4) He was very ambitious and worked hard at gaining a reputation. He became doctor to the Emperor's son and wrote over 100 medical texts.

Galen Publications Buy My Books They're Ace

Galen believed in the Humours and Observation

1) Galen supported the theories of Hippocrates on ethics and observation. He also believed in the four humours (see p.41).
2) He increased his anatomical knowledge (gained from treating wounded gladiators) by dissecting animals. He described the role of the spine in controlling the rest of the body. He couldn't dissect humans or even study a skeleton outside of Alexandria — so he resorted to chance opportunities like a rotting corpse on a gibbet, or a flash flood in a cemetery.
3) Galen was deceived by having to use only animals. He thought that the rete mirabile (a network of blood vessels on the undersurface of the brain) which he found in animals would be found in humans — it wasn't. And he described livers as the wrong shape.
4) He also let his ambition get the better of him. He only recorded his successful cases and he frequently let himself see what he wanted to see — such as tiny pores in the septum of the heart which would let blood pass from the right hand side of the heart to the left.
5) He believed that the blood started life in the liver, then passed around the body picking up various "spirits" (including "pneuma" from the lungs). It did various jobs on the way, finally being consumed rather than recirculated. He thought the nervous system was part of this process.
6) He believed in treatment by opposites. This was based on the idea of balance of the humours.

Galen's Reputation lasted for Centuries

1) Galen had great influence on the doctors in the Arabic world and in medieval Christian Europe.
2) His writings covered all aspects of medicine and many of the books that he wrote survived.
3) His writing was very persuasive and he did not stress the polytheistic (more than one god) side of Roman culture — so he didn't offend the later monotheistic Muslims and Christians. This is one reason why his writings were copied, and so survived.

A Galen of bile — that should cure 'em...

It's pretty hard to understate Galen's importance in medical history. But just stating that won't get you many marks. You need to know why he was so important. Make sure you know why his books were so influential and why he made so many mistakes.

Revision Summary for Sections 1-4

OK, it's question time. They cover most of the really important points. You probably won't be able to answer all of them first time, but don't worry. If you can answer most of them then you're doing pretty well. Your eventual aim should be to answer all of them — and quickly. It's not hard though — it's just a matter of practice. Go through the sections and the questions enough and you'll soon be blitzing them off in no time.

1) Explain the difference between prehistory and history.
2) How might different burial practices affect a culture's level of medical knowledge?
3) What evidence suggests that spiritual cures were attempted in prehistory?
4) a) Name a type of surgery that we know was performed by people in prehistoric societies.
   b) How do we know that people survived this surgery?
5) What geographical feature helped development and communication in ancient Egypt?
6) Why were the gods Sekhmet and Thoth important to Egyptian medicine?
7) Name the Egyptian doctor who was made the god of healing.
8) What is the technical term for the observation of patients and the recognition of symptoms?
9) Explain how the theory and practice of mummification might have affected the development of medicine in ancient Egypt.
10) Name an antiseptic used by the ancient Egyptians.
11) How did the example of the River Nile lead some Egyptians to consider non-spiritual causes for illnesses?
12) What religious ritual might have kept Egyptians more healthy?
13) How were Egyptian toilets emptied?
14) Explain the difference between what it means to be Greek today and what it meant in the 4th century BC.
15) Name the Greek god of healing, and the temples dedicated to him where healing rituals were carried out.
16) What animal was sacred to the Greek god of healing? What part did it play in healing rituals?
17) How did the temples advertise their successes?
18) Give the approximate dates for the birth and death of Hippocrates. Explain his importance.
19) Explain the sequence of actions recommended by Hippocrates to be taken before treatment.
20) What is a regimen?
21) Name the four humours.
22) Where is Alexandria and when was it founded? What was its importance to ancient medicine?
23) Many doctors who worked in Rome weren't from there originally. Where were they from?
24) What was the name of the hospitals set up for wounded soldiers in Rome?
25) Describe an operation historians think the Romans could have carried out successfully.
26) Where was Galen born?
27) Describe two of Galen's major anatomical mistakes.
28) What aspect of Galen's work made it acceptable to Muslims and Christians?

Imperial Collapse and the Dark Ages

The Roman Empire didn't last forever. It weakened, split, then fell. That wasn't good for medicine.

The collapse of the Roman Empire led to the Dark Ages

1) The Roman Empire split into an Eastern Empire and a Western Empire in AD 395. In AD 410 the Goths invaded Italy and Roman troops were withdrawn from provinces, including Britain.

2) The last Roman Emperor in the West was deposed by a German chieftain in AD 476. This led to a very rapid collapse of social organisation, technical skills and academic knowledge.

3) In AD 431 Nestorius, the Christian Patriarch of Jerusalem, was banished for heresy and travelled further East to Persia. There he set up a centre of medical learning that translated the works of Hippocrates and Galen into Arabic.

4) The knowledge of the Greek and Roman eras migrated east and was lost, but not irretrievably, from the western end of the Mediterranean and Europe.

Barbarians and Superstition swept across Europe

1) In England the partly Romanised and partly Christian Celts were gradually overwhelmed by waves of pagan Saxons coming across the North Sea. The Saxons brought with them a return to medical cures based mostly on superstition and magic. So complete was the loss of knowledge that many Saxons believed that the ruins of Roman architecture they saw around them were the work of giants and other mythical beings.

2) Not only did the public health systems of the Romans fall into disrepair, but the people of the Dark Ages lacked the education to understand the value of hygiene, clean water etc. Many of the Roman towns were abandoned in favour of small dispersed farmsteads.

3) The Christian Church re-established itself in Britain from both the east and the west — St. Augustine arrived in Kent in AD 597, and Celtic monks came from Ireland. The Synod of Whitby (AD 663) brought about the dominance of the Roman version of Christianity. This brought Britain into the Church, which provided some of the communication and unity with the rest of Europe that had once been seen in the western Roman Empire.

The Dark Ages — a dark time for medicine...

The fall of the Roman Empire really did have a devastating effect on medicine. This was one of the biggest turning points in the history of medicine — one of those things examiners love to ask you about. Make sure you understand the factors involved in the loss of knowledge — like the superstitious and magical beliefs of the Saxons.

The Arab World

All was not lost though — many Greek medical texts were preserved by the Islamic empire.

Arab doctors maintained and Improved on the Classics

1) Aristotle's four humours, Galen's treatment by opposites and Hippocrates' clinical observation lived on with the Arabists (the name given to those following Arabic schools of medicine).
2) In the ninth century, Hunain ibn Ishaq (also known by his Latin name Johannitius) travelled from Baghdad, the then capital of the Islamic empire, to Byzantium to collect medical texts. He translated these into Arabic.
3) In about AD 910 al-Razi (or Rhazes) distinguished smallpox and measles as separate diseases.
4) Avicenna, a Persian (AD 980 - 1037), wrote the "Canon of Medicine" which brought together the ideas of Aristotle, Galen and Hippocrates. This book was the most important means by which the classical ideas got back into Western Europe.

5) In the 12th century Avenzoar (or Ibn Zuhr) described the parasite that causes scabies and began to question the reliability of Galen — as did Ibn al-Nafis in the 13th century, who suggested (correctly) that the blood flowed from one side of the heart to the other via the lungs — and did not cross the septum. Ibn al-Nafis' work was unknown in the West until the 20th century.
6) Despite Islamic prohibition on human dissection some progress in surgery was made and Albucasis (or Abu al-Qasim, born c.AD 936) wrote a well thought out book describing amputations, the removal of bladder stones and dental surgery — as well as methods for handling fractures and dislocations and the sewing of wounds.

Public Health and Social Organisation were better too

1) The Islamic empire maintained medical schools. Exams for doctors were held in Baghdad from AD 931.
2) Major cities such as Baghdad, Cairo, Damascus and Cordoba had piped water, public baths and hospitals before AD 1000.

Blood crossing the heart — how Nafis that?

Right, so it was the Islamic scholars to the rescue. But they didn't just translate texts — they made some progress, even though they were hindered like many Greeks and Romans by religious objections to human dissection. Make sure you understand the importance of the Islamic governments — especially their introduction of medical schools and exams.

The Arab World

The Arabs didn't just preserve medical learning — they liked to dabble in a bit of <u>alchemy</u> too.

The <u>Arabists were keen on</u> <u>Chemistry</u>

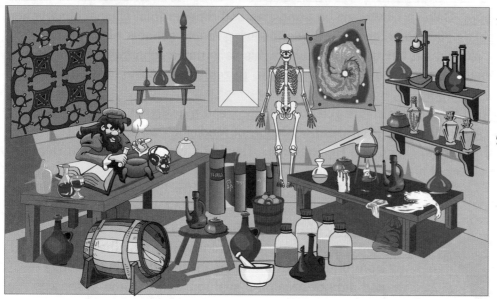

1) Alchemy was the attempt to turn <u>base</u> (ordinary) metals into <u>gold</u> and to discover the elixir of <u>eternal life</u>.

2) <u>Alchemy</u> traces its origins back to the <u>Egyptians</u> and, like much else of ancient and classical learning, it was preserved by the <u>Arabic</u> empire.

3) Unlike modern chemistry, much <u>superstition</u> was included — an unsuccessful experiment was as likely to be blamed on the position of the <u>stars</u> or the spiritual purity of the <u>alchemist</u> as anything else.

4) Even so, Arabic alchemists invented useful <u>techniques</u> such as distillation and sublimation, and prepared useful <u>drugs</u> such as laudanum, benzoin and camphor.

<u>Not everyone in the</u> <u>Islamic</u> <u>world</u> <u>Approved</u>

1) <u>Avicenna's</u> interest in the <u>Greek philosophers</u> (see p.47) produced enemies such as <u>al-Ghazali</u> who wrote '<u>Destruction of the Philosophers</u>' and encouraged a decline in rationalist philosophy in the Islamic world.

2) Avicenna did not believe in <u>personal immortality</u>, or that God was interested in <u>individuals</u>. He did not believe the <u>world creation</u> story either. This goes against the <u>orthodox</u> Islamic tradition. Even so, Avicenna was one of Islam's most influential philosophers.

3) The rise to power of the <u>Mamelukes</u> (slave-soldiers) in <u>1250</u> brought a new hardness to the Islamic world. This was partly in response to the excesses of the <u>Christian crusades</u>.

> So I said, "If you're so good at medicine, stitch that"

The Crusades were a series of wars fought by Christian Europeans against the Muslims. They were an ultimately unsuccessful attempt to retake Jerusalem and the surrounding areas associated with the early history of Christianity.

<u>Alchemy — it's not all chemistry...</u>

Don't ignore alchemy — the search for an <u>elixir</u> of life says a lot about medical knowledge of the time, and of course many useful <u>techniques</u> and <u>drugs</u> were developed.

Medieval Europe

Over the centuries, the old <u>Greek</u> and <u>Roman</u> learning gradually made its way back to the West.

The Church had a big Influence on medieval medicine

1) Scholarship in the early Middle Ages in Europe was dominated by the <u>Catholic Church</u> — which was a massively powerful international organisation.
2) Most educated people had been taught in <u>Church institutions</u>, and the most highly educated people tended to be members of the Church.
3) Many in the Church believed that illness was a <u>punishment for sins</u> — and so the correct response was prayer and penitence (doing things to show you're sorry).
4) Medieval culture had an <u>unquestioning attitude</u> to authoritative texts. So old texts, such as the recovered bits of Galen (see below), were taken to be accurate, even when evidence may have suggested otherwise.
5) The Church did play a role in <u>caring for the sick</u>. Medical care for the poor often came from hospitals set up by monasteries.
6) Famous <u>hospitals</u> like St. Bartholomew's and St. Thomas's in London started life as <u>monastic establishments</u>.

Galen returns to Western Europe

Galen Publications
Buy My Books
They're STILL Ace

1) By about <u>1100</u>, versions of the works of <u>Galen</u> and <u>Hippocrates</u> were coming back into Western <u>Europe</u> bit by bit. <u>Arabic</u> texts based on them, especially <u>Avicenna's Canon</u>, were being translated into <u>Latin</u> in <u>Spain</u> (which was partly Christian and partly Islamic) and <u>Italy</u>. The <u>crusades</u> had also made <u>Europeans</u> aware of the scientific knowledge of the <u>Arabists</u>.
2) About the same time <u>medical schools</u> began to appear in Western Europe, starting with the one in <u>Salerno</u>, Italy. This taught both <u>men and women</u> and had some women professors. Translations of the Arabic versions of <u>Galen</u> and <u>Hippocrates</u> were accepted as <u>absolute truth</u>.

Medicine was dominated by the Four Humours Theory

1) Medieval doctors based their diagnosis and treatments on the theory of the four humours (see p.41). The theory developed into a more and more <u>complex system</u>, taking in the seasons, the stars, different types of food and clothing.
2) Being a doctor meant having studied and learnt from the key ancient texts and the Arabists. This was more important than being experienced in <u>treating people</u>.
3) Other 'healers' such as <u>apothecaries</u> (p.50), who could effectively treat some diseases, but who didn't have such good understanding of the 'theory', weren't as highly regarded.
4) Although <u>human dissection</u> was carried out in the medical schools, it tended to be interpreted in line with the theory of the four humours — although some later medieval doctors began to <u>challenge</u> the traditional understanding of anatomy.

Skeerg! — the return of the Greeks...

You haven't heard the last of those Greeks. It's hard to understate the <u>influence</u> they had in Medieval Europe — but it wasn't all good. There are few better ways to stifle progress than accepting something as the <u>absolute truth</u>.

Medieval Europe

Progress was slow, but medieval medicine did take some important steps forward.

There were some New Developments in medieval medicine

1) More and more schools sprang up (Montpellier, Bologna, Padua, Paris) and human dissection gained acceptance. Debates and new research led to some doubts about the classical texts.

2) Some new techniques were developed including diagnosis by urine samples. Colour and taste were used. This is a good aid to diagnosis, which is why doctors still ask for urine samples from patients today — although modern doctors don't have to rely on taste for analysis.

3) Doctors also believed that the stars caused disease and relied heavily on astrology in making diagnoses and deciding on treatments.

4) In tenth century England, one of the Laws of King Edgar allowed women to train as doctors.

5) As medicine re-emerged as a specialised and high status profession with guilds, it became a male preserve. The Guild of Surgeons got this Law of Edgar revoked in the fifteenth century.

6) The College of Physicians (which later became the Royal College of Physicians) was founded by King Henry VIII in 1518. It licensed doctors, controlling who could officially practise in London, and later in the whole of England. Prospective members had to pass an oral exam to join.

Trained Doctors weren't the only Healers

1) Trained doctors were very expensive. Much of the medicine practised amongst the ordinary people was provided by monasteries, apothecaries and housewife-physicians, using traditional cures (such as bleeding) and experience as their main tools.

2) The Church had access to the Latin texts used by doctors. Religious orders, especially the Hospitallers, were devoted to healing. The Church set up some public hospitals, both general and specialised (e.g. maternity hospitals and leper hospitals) — but there were never enough.

3) Apothecaries sold drugs and medicine — and sometimes advised on their use. The influence of wise-women herbalists on the apothecaries led the Apothecaries' Guild to admit women.

4) The term housewife-physician covers quite a range of people from "wise women" to the lady of the manor, who was often expected to provide medical help and advice to those families on her husband's lands.

Superstition and Faith continued to play a part

1) Medieval people believed that pilgrimages to holy shrines — mainly sites containing the remains of saints — could cure illnesses. Holy water from shrines was thought to help cure sickness. Many people still go to similar sites like Lourdes hoping to be healed.

2) Many doctors had magical and superstitious beliefs — saying certain words when administering treatment. Doctors continued to consult the stars.

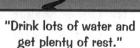

"Drink lots of water and get plenty of rest."

3) Quacks were people without any real medical knowledge who sold medical treatments — that often did more harm than good. They'd sell their wares at fairs and markets.

Abracadabra — and your cold is gone...

Even when there are momentous turning points and important discoveries in the history of medicine, it tends to take a while for improvements to filter down. While rich people would have access to the latest treatments, poor people in the countryside would probably receive the same treatments that their grandparents would have got.

European Surgery and Public Health

In medieval times, surgery was not the respected profession that it is today. Little progress was made.

Anatomy and Surgery — messy work for menials

You just can't get the staff these days!

Liver Mathter?

1) Unlike today when surgeons are the most respected doctors, medieval surgery was held in such low regard that many procedures, like tooth-pulling, were often left to low paid assistants and untrained barber-surgeons (i.e. the local barber).

2) The dissection of corpses as teaching aids began in about 1300 and slowly brought standards of anatomy back to Roman levels and beyond — but progress was slow as the assistants who carried out dissections were required to find what the books and their betters told them to, rather than anything new or different.

3) Surgical treatments were still few and simple, as pain, bleeding and infection made major surgery very risky.

4) Attempts were made at both antiseptics and anaesthetics, but they were not widely adopted. No notion of infection by germs existed. The use of wine as a mild antiseptic by Hugh of Lucca and his son Theoderic in the early 13th century was prompted by empirical observation (they just noticed that it worked). A recipe for an anaesthetic by John of Arderne in 1376 included hemlock, opium and henbane (a relative of deadly nightshade). In carefully controlled doses this may have worked — but was very likely to kill.

Public Health measures were almost Non-existent

1) As towns and cities began to reappear they lacked the Romans' central organisation, and the willingness of the wealthy to provide water and sewerage.

Water — never touch it. Unholy stuff!

2) Only the monasteries made much real effort to provide clean running water and effective toilets. Even the wealthy in the towns had to rely on inadequate cesspits and adjacent wells — or water courses that were little more than open sewers. Those without a cesspit frequently disposed of waste into the street in the hope that it would wash away.

3) It is little wonder that people found it healthier to drink wine and beer or buy water brought in on pack animals from outside the towns. Most wealthy houses and monasteries brewed their own beer — providing large quantities of low alcohol "small beer" for servants. The brewing process involves boiling, which sterilises the liquid.

4) Some town corporations (councils) tried to regulate against the most disgusting practices. But without real understanding of the risks, there was little will and less financial support to do anything effective.

The Middle Ages — beer today, bone tomorrow...

Medieval doctors and surgeons might have followed Greek and Roman practice — but alas, the same wasn't true of their governments. Medieval towns were filthy — but in most cases nothing was done. Make sure you understand why. Try comparing medieval Europe with the Roman Empire, and try to explain the similarities and differences — it's excellent exam practice.

The Black Death

Medieval conditions were a tad <u>unwholesome</u>. It was only a matter of time before disaster struck.

Armageddon in the 14th century — the Black Death

1) The <u>Black Death</u> was a series of <u>plagues</u> that first swept Europe in the mid <u>14th century</u>. Two illnesses were involved: <u>pneumonic plague</u>, spread by coughs and sneezes (airborne), and <u>bubonic plague</u>, spread by black rat flea bites. <u>Black rats</u> were carried overseas by <u>ships</u>.

2) Black Death arrived in <u>Britain</u> in <u>1348</u>. Its victims were struck down suddenly and mostly died. Between a <u>third</u> and a <u>half</u> of the population were killed. From <u>1347-1351</u>, <u>75 million</u> people died from it worldwide. Later outbreaks included the <u>Great Plague of London</u> in <u>1665</u>.

> This devastation affected the <u>labour market</u> and patterns of land ownership. It affected the ability of the country to raise armies. It changed use of farm land. It was partly responsible for the <u>abandonment</u> of many villages.

The plague went from Bad to Worse

1) <u>Bubonic plague</u> was the first to strike in 1348. Sufferers were hit by <u>exhaustion</u>, <u>headaches</u> and a <u>high temperature</u>. This was followed by the rise of <u>big swellings</u> in the groin, armpits or on the neck — these are the <u>buboes</u>, which give the disease its name. Some survived the disease, but many died <u>around a week</u> after first being infected.

2) The plague turned into <u>pneumonic plague</u>, which is far <u>more deadly</u>. This attacks the <u>lungs</u> — making it <u>painful</u> and <u>difficult</u> to <u>breathe</u>. Other symptoms included coughing up blood. Pneumonic plague kills its victims within a <u>couple of days</u>.

Many people thought the Plague was a Punishment

1) People thought the plague was a <u>judgement from God</u>, or caused by the <u>planets</u>. Some thought it was caused by <u>foul air</u>. Others looked for people to blame, such as the <u>Jews</u> or the <u>nobility</u>.

2) Many thought the <u>end of the world</u> was near and looked for signs of <u>Armageddon</u>.

3) Some people tried to appease the <u>Wrath of God</u> by becoming <u>flagellants</u>, whipping themselves and praying.

It was a Dangerous Time to be a doctor

1) It took a very <u>brave</u> person to help someone with the disease.

2) Some doctors and clergymen did try to help and took all the <u>precautions</u> they could think of. Strong smelling <u>herbs</u> were used to counter the <u>foul airs</u> believed to carry the disease.

3) All-over <u>suits</u> were worn which might have filtered out airborne germs and provided a temporary barrier against fleas. Ships were made to wait <u>40 days</u> before landing — the word "<u>quarantine</u>" comes from the Italian "<u>quaranta</u>", meaning 40.

Don't plague aims — this black death is serious stuff...

Not much fun this page, I'm afraid — but that doesn't mean you can ignore it. The essential point is that medieval Europe was faced with something it <u>didn't understand</u> — and something it was <u>helpless</u> to prevent. And since they didn't have an understanding of the <u>cause</u>, not many lessons were learned — so it's no surprise the plague <u>returned</u> later.

Renaissance and Reformation

A return to classical ideas and the reformation of the church were <u>turning points</u> for medicine.

The Renaissance brought a sharper focus on the Classics

1) The <u>Renaissance</u> (which means "rebirth") is the name given to the changes which started in the cities of Northern Italy during the <u>14th century</u>, and spread throughout Europe over the next <u>two hundred years</u>.

2) It started by embracing the close study of <u>classical texts</u>. It was <u>critical</u> of old translations.

3) In medicine there was a greater interest in how the human body <u>worked</u> based on <u>direct observation</u> and <u>dissection</u>.

4) The Renaissance saw the emergence of <u>science</u> as we know it today from the magic and mysticism of the medieval alchemists and astrologers. <u>The Royal Society</u>, Britain's most prestigious scientific body, was founded in <u>1660</u>. It had patronage from King Charles II which gave it <u>high status</u>. Science began to oust superstition from medicine.

5) <u>Renaissance Man</u> is an important concept — the idea that a well educated person should be proficient in <u>science and art</u>. People like Leonardo da Vinci were brilliant at both — and wouldn't have seen any clear division. Artists attended <u>dissections</u> of human corpses and wrote on scientific subjects using <u>wonderful illustrations</u>.

6) The return of the original Greek texts of the works of the great <u>classical authors</u> such as <u>Hippocrates</u> and <u>Galen</u> led to renewed faith in the four humours theory and treatment by opposites.

Leonardo da Vinci

It was a time of change for the Church too...

1) In the 16th century some <u>religious thinkers</u> felt that the Catholic Church had become corrupt and got too far away from the <u>teachings of the Bible</u>.

2) Men such as <u>Martin Luther</u> wanted the Church to be <u>reformed</u> and for the Bible to be translated into <u>modern languages</u> that ordinary people could understand.

3) This movement became known as the <u>Reformation</u>. <u>Protestant</u> Churches, independent of the Catholic Church, spread across Europe.

4) The Reformation was a time when traditional religious <u>authority</u> was <u>challenged</u> and <u>knowledge</u> spread to a <u>greater range</u> of people — this ethos influenced the wider world and had an impact on the development of medicine.

There were Mixed Reactions to the New Ideas

1) There was <u>resistance</u> to the new ideas of the Renaissance and the Reformation. The scientist <u>Galileo Galilei</u> was persecuted by the <u>Inquisition</u> (a Catholic organisation set up to root out unorthodox beliefs) in <u>1633</u>.

2) 'Renaissance Man' <u>Paracelsus</u> began his lecturing career in <u>Basel</u> in <u>1527</u> by burning one of <u>Galen's</u> books and calling him a liar and <u>Avicenna</u> a kitchen master. More importantly he rejected the idea of the <u>four humours</u>. He gave his lectures in <u>German</u> instead of the academic language of <u>Latin</u>, and opened them to anyone who wanted to attend — including <u>barber-surgeons</u>.

The Inquisition

Come in and talk about Science. BYO kindling.

Paracelsus? I prefer aspirin myself...

Lots of background stuff here you need to know. The <u>Renaissance</u> was a big <u>turning point</u> for medicine — make sure you know <u>why</u>. Whatever you do, don't get those "<u>Re</u>" words confused.

Public Health, War & the Plague of London

Although medical knowledge had advanced since the Middle Ages, life for many people was still pretty grim, and public health was poor.

Public Health was made worse by War

1) The Renaissance was a very violent period. Religious differences led to many wars. Large mercenary armies fought in long inconclusive conflicts, such as the Italian Wars and the Thirty Years' War (1618-1648).
2) Populations were beginning to increase in the towns and cities, placing more strain on the available clean water supplies and sewage disposal systems.
3) Warfare gobbled up resources, destroyed crops and bottled people up in besieged towns without enough food. Starvation, camp fever (Typhoid), plague and sexually transmitted diseases followed the armies around the continent, killing far more than muskets or cannon.
4) Homelessness and those permanently disabled by war put unsustainable pressures on parish structures intended for poor relief.
5) Naval power and the science of navigation improved worldwide communication. Here is one of the few examples of communication as a negative factor. Diseases common in Europe like smallpox, measles and syphilis were spread to North and South America, while cholera was on its way to Europe from the East.

The Great Plague hit London in 1665

1) This was the worst of the not infrequent reappearances of the Black Death (see p.52).
2) The death toll in London was about 100 000 and many fled from the city.
3) Some efforts were made to control the spread of the disease. Afflicted households were locked in and red crosses were painted on their doors with the words, "Lord have mercy upon us." Carts organised by the authorities roamed the city to the now infamous cry of "Bring out your dead!" collecting corpses for mass burial in "plague pits".

DEAD! I said, "Bring out your DEAD!"

4) Such measures showed that people realised that the disease was contagious, but they still didn't understand about germs.
5) Doctors, chemists and priests were worse affected than average because it was to them that the sick went for help.
6) The Great Fire of London in 1666 effectively sterilised large parts of London, killing the plague bacteria.

Europe was once more plagued by plague...

What joy, what fun. More gory bits to learn. Remember to learn about new problems and failures as well as the cures and developments. If you want the right atmosphere for this page go and watch 'The Last Valley' with Omar Sharif and Michael Caine (as the only Cockney-German Mercenary in the Thirty Years' War). Now scribble down those facts and enjoy...

Printing and Anatomy Books

Pressed for time? Don't ignore this page — it's important...

Printing — one of the greatest inventions of all time

1) <u>Johann Gutenberg</u> introduced printing to Europe in <u>1454</u>. This invention accelerated the <u>rate of progress</u> in medicine and everything else. It made it much easier for ideas to spread and be debated widely. <u>William Caxton</u> set up the first <u>British</u> printing press in <u>1476</u> in Westminster Abbey.

2) Making a single copy of a book <u>by hand</u> could take many months or even years for a copyist. Books were therefore very <u>rare</u> and precious before printing. New ideas would have to be <u>thoroughly accepted</u> before anyone would go to the bother of copying them by hand.

3) Between <u>1500</u> and <u>1531</u> more complete copies of <u>Galen's</u> works, especially '<u>On the Use of Parts</u>' and '<u>On Anatomical Procedures</u>' came out of the East, were translated into Latin and published by use of the <u>printing press</u>. The most common version of Galen used before that was <u>Mondino de Luzzi's</u> book '<u>Anatomy</u>' of <u>1316</u>, based on fragments of '<u>On the Use of Parts</u>'.

Vesalius wrote anatomy books with Accurate Diagrams

Some people will steal anything!

1) <u>Vesalius</u> was born in <u>1514</u> and studied anatomy in <u>Louvain</u> and <u>Paris</u>. He was allowed to perform <u>dissections</u>, but not to boil up bodies to get <u>skeletons</u>. He pinched a rather ripe body from a <u>gibbet</u> — dirty job, but someone's got to do it.

2) He became professor of <u>surgery</u> and <u>anatomy</u> at Padua.

3) He did his own dissections rather than employing a <u>menial demonstrator</u>, and he wrote books based on his observations using <u>accurate diagrams</u> to illustrate his work. The most important were '<u>Tabulae Sex</u>' ('<u>six</u> pictures', <u>1538</u>) and '<u>The Fabric of the Human Body</u>' (<u>1543</u>).

4) His illustrations were carefully <u>annotated</u> so that he could refer to specific parts in the text. He oversaw <u>all stages</u> in the production.

5) His work served to point out some of <u>Galen's</u> mistakes. In the second edition of 'The Fabric' Vesalius said there were no holes in the <u>septum</u> of the heart — and his successor, <u>Colombo</u>, said (<u>1559</u>) that blood went from one side of the heart to the other <u>via the lungs</u>. This was 300 years after <u>Ibn al-Nafis</u> (see p.47).

I'm bleeding right!

No you're bleeding not!

Hey PRESSto — surgery by the book...

<u>Communication</u> is of course one of the key factors you might be asked about — and for good reason. Remember that lack of communication was probably the biggest thing <u>hindering</u> the development of medicine through the Middle Ages. The <u>printing press</u> changed all that. Think how much harder it would have been for <u>Vesalius</u> to make a difference without it.

Paré and Harvey

Bored? Harvey look at this...

Paré was forced to Improvise

1) Ambroise Paré was a barber-surgeon born in 1510. Surgery was still a low status profession. Paré worked for a public hospital, then became an army surgeon.

2) At this time the severed blood vessels left by amputation were sealed by burning their ends using a red hot iron (cauterisation). This caused extreme discomfort for the already stressed patient. Paré invented the method of tying off vessels with threads (ligatures). He also designed quite sophisticated artificial legs.

3) Gunshot wounds caused infection more often than arrow or blade wounds. We now know this is because a bullet carries soiled cloth and skin into the wound and produces a great deal of dead tissue encouraging infection. At the time people thought that bullets were poisoned by the gunpowder. The standard treatment was to use the hot iron again — or even to pour boiling oil into the wound. This may have worked in some cases, but would have caused more harm than good.

4) During one battle Paré ran out of oil and resorted, by chance, to a simple cool salve instead. To his surprise the patients treated that way did better than the ones scalded with the oil.

5) Eventually he became surgeon to the King of France, but his ideas were resisted by doctors who thought that a lowly surgeon should not be listened to. It took the King's support to gain his ideas some acceptance.

War is Hell! The red hot iron, the boiling oil — and that's just what we do to our own side!

Harvey discovered the Circulation of the blood

1) William Harvey was born in 1578 and studied medicine and anatomy at Padua. He then worked in London as a doctor and a lecturer at the Royal College of Surgeons, before becoming Royal Physician to James I and Charles I.

2) He did comparative studies (c.1615) on animals and humans. He realised that he could observe living animal hearts in action and his findings would also apply to humans.

3) Galen had thought that the blood was formed, carried to the tissues and then consumed. Harvey realised this was wrong. His logic for suggesting circulation was that too much blood was being pumped out of the heart for it to be continually formed and consumed — so it must be going round and round.

4) He also identified the difference between arteries and veins, which built on the discoveries of Erasistratus (c.250 BC) — and he noticed that blood changes colour as it passes through the lungs.

5) Although Harvey's work was very important and a turning point in anatomy, it didn't radically change the practice of surgery. Bleeding continued to be performed and blood transfusions were not generally successful until the discovery of blood groups in 1900.

Oil be darned — this could salve a few lives...

Two key developments here, both due to the brilliance of individuals. Harvey and other doctors could only observe dead human hearts — for obvious reasons — so the heart was badly understood. It took Harvey's cunning to get round the problem. Don't forget that Paré needed the King's help to get his message across — a good example of the effect of social attitudes.

Revision Summary for Sections 5-6

That's another big chunk covered so it's time for more questions. Most of these are fairly straightforward tests of what you know. Keep on going through them until you can do the whole lot without checking — not even one sneaky peek.

1) Where was the meeting that brought Britain into the Roman Catholic Church?
2) Name the Arabists associated with:
   a) the collection and translation of Greek texts   b) smallpox   c) the 'Canon of Medicine'
   d) scabies   e) the heart and lungs.
3) Describe the developments made in public health and medical training in Arabic cities by AD 1000.
4) What was the primary aim of the alchemists? What did they actually achieve?
5) Why did Avicenna's work provoke hostility amongst some scholars of the time?
6) Discuss the effect of the Roman Catholic Church on medicine in the medieval period.
7) Name a book that was important in bringing the ideas of Hippocrates and Galen back into Western Europe.
8) What was the general attitude towards the writings of the classical scholars, such as Galen, in medieval Europe?
9) What did one of the Laws of King Edgar allow women to do?
10) When was the College of Physicians founded?
11) Were university-trained doctors the most common medical practitioners available to the people of medieval Britain? What alternatives were there?
12) Who usually carried out anatomical dissection and surgery? Were they respected people?
13) What was used as a mild antiseptic in the early 13th century?
14) When and how did the Black Death reach Britain and what proportion of the population died?
15) What causes were suggested for the Black Death?
16) What practical and spiritual measures did people take in response to the Black Death?
17) Name the important scientific institution founded in 1660.
18) Explain what the term 'Renaissance Man' means.
19) How did Paracelsus accelerate the rate of change in medical theory?
20) In what year was the Great Plague of London?
21) How were houses which had been affected by the plague marked out?
22) In what year was Vesalius born? Name two of his books.
23) Why did Paré experiment with a cool salve for battlefield injuries?
24) What did Harvey discover about the circulation of the blood? How big an effect did his discoveries have on surgery at the time?

The Age of Enlightenment

Jenner's <u>vaccination</u> was a landmark in the development of <u>preventative medicine</u>.

Lady Montagu *introduced Inoculation from Turkey*

1) In the <u>18th century</u>, <u>smallpox</u> was a major killer. The disease was frequently <u>fatal</u> and usually left any survivors badly <u>scarred</u> and <u>disfigured</u>.
2) <u>Lady Mary Wortley Montagu</u> learnt about <u>inoculation</u> in <u>Turkey</u> and introduced it to Britain. Inoculation had arrived in Turkey from <u>China</u>.
3) Montagu discovered that a healthy person could be <u>immunised</u> against smallpox using <u>pus</u> from the sores of someone suffering with a <u>mild form</u> of the disease.

A thread <u>soaked in pus</u> was drawn through a <u>small cut</u> in the person to be inoculated. After a mild reaction, they were <u>immune</u> to smallpox.

4) Unfortunately inoculation sometimes led to <u>full-blown</u> smallpox and death. The fear of smallpox led people to take the <u>risk</u> of inoculation. Doctors could become <u>rich</u> doing inoculations.

Jenner *was very interested in* Milkmaids

1) <u>Edward Jenner</u> (b. <u>1749</u>) was a country doctor in <u>Gloucestershire</u>. He heard that <u>milkmaids</u> didn't get smallpox, but they did catch the much milder <u>cowpox</u>.
2) Using careful <u>scientific methods</u> Jenner investigated and discovered that it was true that people who had had <u>cowpox</u> didn't get <u>smallpox</u>.
3) In <u>1796</u> Jenner was ready to <u>test</u> his theory. He took a small boy called <u>James Phipps</u> and injected him with <u>pus</u> from the sores of <u>Sarah Nelmes</u>, a milkmaid with <u>cowpox</u>. Jenner then injected him with <u>smallpox</u>. James didn't catch the disease.
4) The Latin for cow, <u>vacca</u>, gives us the word <u>vaccination</u>.

Jenner *became* World Famous, *but not everyone was happy*

1) <u>Smallpox</u> was taken to <u>America</u> by European settlers — Jenner's <u>vaccinations</u> made him famous even amongst the <u>Native Americans</u>, who sent a delegation to England to thank him.
2) In <u>1802</u> and <u>1806</u> Parliament gave Jenner <u>£10 000</u> and <u>£20 000</u> respectively — equivalent to <u>millions</u> today.
3) Vaccination was made <u>free</u> for infants in <u>1840</u> and <u>compulsory</u> in <u>1853</u>.
4) Some people were <u>opposed</u> to vaccination. Some doctors who gave the older type of inoculation saw it as a threat to their livelihood, and many people were worried about giving themselves a disease from <u>cows</u>.

If only there was a vaccination against exams...

Vaccination is a brilliant example of how <u>government action</u> can improve public health — by 1979 smallpox had been completely <u>eradicated</u> worldwide. Excellent stuff. Don't forget that the <u>causes</u> of disease weren't understood, so how vaccination worked was a mystery until much later. Its development was solely based on Jenner's <u>observation</u> and <u>clear thinking</u>.

Developments in Nursing

Horrific conditions during the Crimean War (1854-1856) brought two nurses to the public's attention.

The "Lady with the Lamp" changed nursing

F. Nightingale

1) Florence Nightingale (1820-1910) brought a new sense of discipline and professionalism to a job that had a very bad reputation at the time.
2) She became a nurse despite the opposition of her family, and studied in Europe from 1849.
3) The Crimean War broke out in March 1854. The use of telegraphic communications by war correspondents to get stories home fast encouraged people to have opinions and comment.
4) Horror stories emerged about the Barrack Hospital in Scutari, where the British wounded were being treated.
5) Sidney Herbert, who was both the Secretary of War and a friend of the Nightingale family, requested that Florence went to Scutari to sort out the nursing care in the hospital.
6) Despite opposition from the military, Florence went — taking with her 38 hand-picked nurses. Before she arrived, the death rate in the hospital stood at 42%. Two years later it had fallen to just 2%. This was partly the result of huge improvements Florence made to ward hygiene.

Florence Nightingale returned with a Mission

1) Florence Nightingale used her fame to help her change the face of nursing forever.
2) Her book, 'Notes on Nursing', explained her methods — it was the standard textbook for generations of nurses.
3) The public raised £44 000 to help her train nurses, and she set up the Nightingale School of Nursing in St. Thomas' Hospital, London. Discipline and attention to detail were important.
4) By 1900 there were 64 000 trained nurses in Britain, from colleges across the country.
5) The 1919 Registration of Nurses Act made training compulsory for nurses.
6) It wasn't until 1960 that men were admitted to the Royal College of Nursing.

"Mother Seacole" also nursed in the Crimea

1) Mary Jane Seacole (1805-1881) learnt nursing from her mother, who ran a boarding house for invalid soldiers in Kingston, Jamaica.
2) In 1854, she came to England to volunteer as a nurse in the Crimean War. She was rejected — possibly on racist grounds — but went anyway, paying for her own passage.
3) Financing herself by selling goods to the soldiers and travellers, she nursed soldiers on the battlefields and built the British Hotel — a small group of makeshift buildings that served as a hospital, shop and canteen for the soldiers.
4) She couldn't find work as a nurse in England after the war and went bankrupt — though she did receive support due to the press interest in her story. She wrote an autobiography.

Like it or lamp it, you've got to learn it...

When you think of turning points, it's so easy to just think of watershed discoveries — and forget about things like nursing, which have often made just as much difference. Like with Paré, Nightingale's work is an example of how wars sometimes help lead to advances in healthcare.

Germs and the Fight Against Them

In France, Pasteur had the germ of an idea.

1857 — the start of the War on Germs

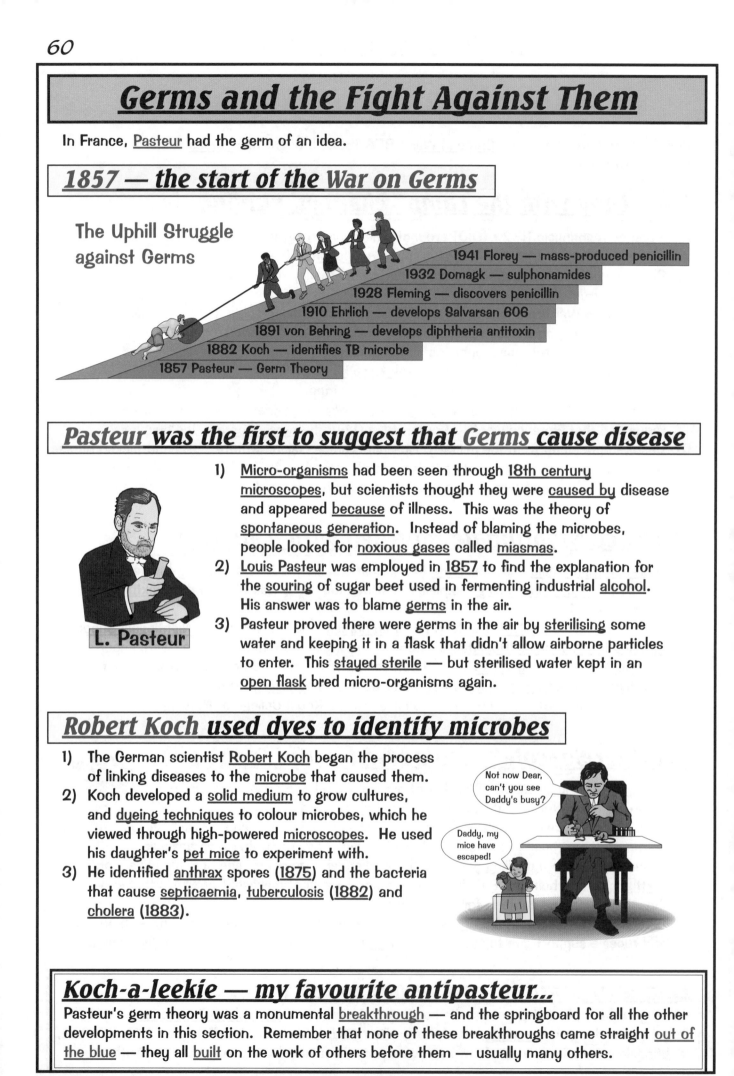

The Uphill Struggle against Germs

1941 Florey — mass-produced penicillin
1932 Domagk — sulphonamides
1928 Fleming — discovers penicillin
1910 Ehrlich — develops Salvarsan 606
1891 von Behring — develops diphtheria antitoxin
1882 Koch — identifies TB microbe
1857 Pasteur — Germ Theory

Pasteur was the first to suggest that Germs cause disease

L. Pasteur

1) Micro-organisms had been seen through 18th century microscopes, but scientists thought they were caused by disease and appeared because of illness. This was the theory of spontaneous generation. Instead of blaming the microbes, people looked for noxious gases called miasmas.

2) Louis Pasteur was employed in 1857 to find the explanation for the souring of sugar beet used in fermenting industrial alcohol. His answer was to blame germs in the air.

3) Pasteur proved there were germs in the air by sterilising some water and keeping it in a flask that didn't allow airborne particles to enter. This stayed sterile — but sterilised water kept in an open flask bred micro-organisms again.

Robert Koch used dyes to identify microbes

1) The German scientist Robert Koch began the process of linking diseases to the microbe that caused them.

2) Koch developed a solid medium to grow cultures, and dyeing techniques to colour microbes, which he viewed through high-powered microscopes. He used his daughter's pet mice to experiment with.

3) He identified anthrax spores (1875) and the bacteria that cause septicaemia, tuberculosis (1882) and cholera (1883).

Not now Dear, can't you see Daddy's busy?

Daddy, my mice have escaped!

Koch-a-leekie — my favourite antipasteur...

Pasteur's germ theory was a monumental breakthrough — and the springboard for all the other developments in this section. Remember that none of these breakthroughs came straight out of the blue — they all built on the work of others before them — usually many others.

Vaccines and Antitoxins

Fuelled by ambition and personal rivalries, the race for further discoveries was on.

Pasteur found the Vaccine for Chicken Cholera

1) Hearing of Koch's work, Pasteur came out of retirement in 1877 and started to compete in the race to find new microbes and combat them.
2) Many other scientists joined this new field of bacteriology.
3) Pasteur looked for cures to anthrax and chicken cholera. Both he and Koch worked with large teams of scientists in this Franco-German competition for national prestige. Charles Chamberland was in Pasteur's team.
4) One day Chamberland was told to inject some chickens with chicken cholera, but it was the day before his holiday and he forgot (as you do). He left the cholera culture on his desk and injected the chickens when he returned.

Where are you going with that needle?

5) The chickens survived. They tried again with some newly cultured cholera, but the chickens still survived.
6) They worked out that the cholera had been weakened by being left on the desk for a few days, and that the weakened (attenuated) cholera had made the chickens immune — in the same way that Jenner's cowpox vaccine had worked for smallpox. Chamberland's error had produced a chance discovery.

Vaccines for Anthrax and Rabies soon followed

1) Pasteur's team then managed to produce an attenuated version of the anthrax spore that would make sheep immune. They demonstrated this in a public experiment in 1881.
2) Next on their hit list was rabies. Emile Roux had used dried rabbit spines to discover how long the rabies microbe remained dangerous. Pasteur borrowed (OK, nicked) Roux's idea to create a series of inoculations of increasing virulence (liveliness). He hoped these would lead to immunity.

3) In 1885 a distraught woman arrived with her son, who had been horribly bitten by a rabid dog. Knowing that the child was bound to die if nothing was done, Pasteur agreed to try out the new treatment on him. Fortunately, the treatment worked.

More help came for those Already Ill...

1) The diphtheria germ had been discovered by Edwin Klebs in 1883.
2) Friedrich Loeffler cultured the germs and thought that their effect on people was due to a poison or toxin they produced. Emile Roux proved Loeffler right.
3) In 1891 Emil von Behring produced an antitoxin or serum — a substance that cancels out the toxins produced by germs — from the blood of animals that had just recovered from diphtheria. This could be used to reduce the effect of the disease.

Goodbye to germs — Pasteur la vista, baby...

Pasteur and Koch were legendary rivals. This was partly because Pasteur was French and Koch German — the two were working around the time of the Franco-Prussian War (1870-1871), in which France suffered a crushing defeat to Germany. The pair's rivalry helped to spur the two scientists on — each wanted to be responsible for making the greatest discovery.

Antibodies and Penicillin

The diphtheria antitoxin was only the first of many effective <u>cures</u> found by modern science.

Paul Ehrlich _found a chemical treatment for Syphilis_

<u>Antibodies</u> were identified as a <u>natural defence</u> mechanism of the body against <u>germs</u>. It was known that antibodies only attacked <u>specific microbes</u> — so they were nicknamed <u>magic bullets</u>. In 1889, <u>Paul Ehrlich</u> set out to find chemicals that could act as <u>synthetic antibodies</u>.

1) First, Ehrlich discovered <u>dyes</u> that could kill the <u>malaria</u> and <u>sleeping sickness</u> germs.
2) Then, in <u>1905</u>, the <u>spirochete bacterium</u> that causes the sexually transmitted disease <u>syphilis</u> was identified.
3) For many years <u>arsenic</u> and <u>mercury</u> had been used with some success to cure syphilis. Unfortunately both are <u>poisonous</u>, so it was a fine line between <u>curing and killing</u>.

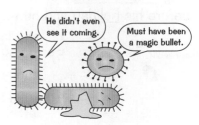

4) Ehrlich and his team decided to search for an <u>arsenic compound</u> that was a <u>magic bullet</u> for syphilis. They hoped it would target the spirochetes <u>without</u> poisoning the rest of the body.
5) Over <u>600</u> compounds were tried, but none seemed to work.
6) In 1909, <u>Sahachiro Hata</u> joined the team. He <u>rechecked</u> the results and found that compound <u>number 606</u> actually appeared to work. It was first used on a human in <u>1911</u> under the trade name <u>Salvarsan 606</u>.

Fleming _discovered Penicillin — the first Antibiotic_

1) The discovery of <u>penicillin</u> is a great example of a <u>chance</u> finding helping science.
2) <u>Alexander Fleming</u> saw many soldiers die of septic wounds caused by <u>staphylococcal</u> bacteria when he was working in an army hospital during the <u>First World War</u>.
3) Searching for a cure he identified the <u>antiseptic</u> substance in tears, <u>lysozyme</u>, in <u>1922</u> — but this only worked on <u>some</u> germs.

4) One day in <u>1928</u> he came to clean up some old <u>culture dishes</u> on which he had been growing <u>staphylococci</u> for his experiments. By chance, a <u>fungal spore</u> had landed and grown on one of the dishes.
5) What caught Fleming's eye was that the <u>colonies</u> of staphylococci around the <u>mould</u> had stopped growing. The <u>fungus</u> was identified as _Penicillium notatum_. It produced a <u>substance</u> that killed <u>bacteria</u>. The substance was given the name <u>penicillin</u>.
6) Fleming was unable to take his work further. The <u>industrial production</u> of penicillin still needed to be developed.

Ehrlich in the morning, when the dye was dawning...

Paul Ehrlich's work was basically <u>trial and error</u>, based on a hunch. The fact that so many different compounds were tested is some measure of his <u>perseverance</u> — a key quality of all these scientists. <u>Chance</u> played a big role in Ehrlich's discovery, but probably not as much as in <u>Fleming's</u>. When you think you know the facts, cover the page, note them down, then <u>check</u>.

Sulphonamides and Penicillin

There were lots more surprises to come — including another <u>dye-hard</u> and <u>pure penicillin</u>.

Gerhard Domagk <u>found a dye that stopped</u> Streptococci

1) In <u>1932</u>, <u>Gerhard Domagk</u> found that a red dye, <u>prontosil</u>, stopped the <u>streptococcus</u> microbe from multiplying in mice — <u>without</u> being poisonous to the mice.

> Streptococcus caused a frequently <u>fatal blood poisoning</u> that could be contracted from very minor <u>wounds</u>. Many surgeons contracted it after cutting themselves in the operating theatre.

Just tell them you've been on holiday to Majorca.

2) In <u>1935</u>, Domagk's daughter pricked herself with a needle and caught the disease. Afraid she would <u>die</u>, Domagk gave her a <u>large dose</u> of <u>prontosil</u>. The girl turned <u>bright red</u>, but recovered.

3) The active ingredient of prontosil was identified as a <u>sulphonamide</u> by <u>French</u> scientists. A whole group of <u>drugs</u> based on sulphonamides followed, including <u>M&B 693</u>, which worked on <u>pneumonia</u> without turning you any strange colour.

4) Sadly more serious <u>side-effects</u> were discovered later. Sulphonamide drugs can damage your <u>liver and kidneys</u>.

Florey and Chain <u>found a way to</u> Purify Penicillin

1) Being a <u>natural product</u>, penicillin needed <u>purifying</u>. The breakthrough was made by <u>Howard Florey's</u> team in <u>Oxford</u> between <u>1938</u> and <u>1940</u>. <u>Ernst Chain</u>, a member of the team, devised the <u>freeze-drying</u> technique which was an important part of the purification process.

2) At first Florey and Chain didn't have the resources to produce penicillin in large amounts. They made penicillin for their first <u>clinical trial</u> by growing *Penicillium notatum* in every container they could find in their lab. The patient began to recover, only to die when the penicillin <u>ran out</u>.

3) <u>Florey</u> knew that <u>penicillin</u> could be vital in treating the <u>wounds</u> being received by <u>soldiers</u> at the time (<u>WWII</u>). British <u>chemical firms</u> were too busy making <u>explosives</u> to start mass production — so he went to <u>America</u>.

4) American firms were not keen to help — until America joined the war in <u>1941</u>. By <u>1944</u> <u>mass production</u> was sufficient for the needs of the <u>military medics</u>.

5) <u>Fleming</u>, <u>Florey</u> and <u>Chain</u> were awarded the <u>Nobel Prize</u> in <u>1945</u>.

A cure for all ills? — not Fleming likely...

Yet another example of <u>war</u> helping to advance medicine. And another use of <u>dyes</u>. The stuff on <u>penicillin's</u> really important. Make sure you understand the <u>effect</u> it had on medicine. But don't forget it was no use in minute quantities — so <u>technology</u> was essential for its production. Just think what a difference that would have made in <u>earlier centuries</u>.

Anaesthetics

Pain, bleeding and infection were the three bugbears of surgery.

Anaesthetics *made life easier for all concerned*

Natural drugs like alcohol, opium and mandrake had long been used to reduce pain — but effective anaesthetics that didn't make the patient very ill were more difficult to produce.

1) Nitrous oxide (laughing gas) was identified as a possible anaesthetic by Humphry Davy in 1799 — but he was ignored by surgeons of the time.

2) The gas had been relegated to use as a fairground novelty before Horace Wells suggested its use in dentistry. He did a public demonstration in 1845, but had the bad luck to pick a patient unaffected by nitrous oxide — it was again ignored.

3) In 1842, Crawford Long discovered the anaesthetic qualities of ether — but he didn't publish his work.

4) The first public demonstration of ether as an anaesthetic was carried out in 1846 by William Morton.

5) Ether is an irritant and is also fairly explosive, so using it in this way was risky. In 1847 James Simpson experimented on himself to find an alternative. He discovered the effects of chloroform.

6) Chloroform was widely used in operating theatres and to reduce pain during childbirth — but it sometimes affected the heart, causing patients to die suddenly.

What was it we were looking for again?

Dr Simpson and his team experimenting in his dining room.

7) General anaesthesia (complete unconsciousness) is risky, so local anaesthesia (numbing of the part being treated) is better for many operations. In 1884, William Halsted investigated the use of cocaine as a local anaesthetic. Unfortunately, his self-experimentation led to a severe cocaine addiction.

Early Anaesthetics actually led to a Rise in death rates

1) Some people were suspicious of doctors using anaesthetics — or even objected on religious grounds. Others were afraid of side effects and the dangers of overdose.

2) Surgeons were keen to perform more and more complicated operations because an unconscious patient was cooperative and the surgeon could take longer over his work.

3) As the dangers of bleeding and infection had not been overcome, the attempts at more complicated surgery actually led to increased death rates amongst patients. The period between 1846 and 1870 is sometimes called the "Black Period" of surgery.

4) Modern anaesthetists use complicated mixtures to produce muscle relaxation or paralysis as well as unconsciousness.

Anaesthetics — learn your stuff and it won't hurt a bit...

Anaesthetics were definitely a major advance, but don't forget about that grisly "Black Period" — and what caused it. You should be able to recite the facts in your sleep, but you're not allowed anaesthetic for the exam. If you know it all, it won't be too painful.

Antisepsis and Asepsis

Luckily, methods to <u>reduce infection</u> soon followed.

Antisepsis **and** Asepsis **reduce infection**

There are two main approaches to <u>reducing infection</u> during an operation:

> 1) <u>Antiseptic</u> methods are used to <u>kill germs</u> that get near surgical wounds.
> 2) <u>Aseptic</u> surgical methods aim to <u>stop any germs</u> getting near the wound.

Joseph Lister **pioneered the use of** Antiseptics

1) <u>Ignaz Semmelweis</u> (1818-1865) had used <u>chloride of lime</u> solution as a <u>hand wash</u> for doctors to control the spread of <u>puerperal</u> fever, an infection suffered by many women following childbirth. However, it was very <u>unpleasant</u>, so wasn't widely used.
2) <u>Joseph Lister</u> had seen <u>carbolic acid</u> sprays used in <u>sewage works</u> to keep down the smell. He tried this in the <u>operating theatre</u> in the early <u>1860s</u> and saw reduced <u>infection rates</u>. Having heard about the <u>germ theory</u> in <u>1865</u>, he realised that germs could be in the air and on surgical instruments and people's hands. He started using carbolic acid on <u>instruments</u> and <u>bandages</u>. This produced further improvements.
3) <u>Carbolic acid</u> is unpleasant to get on your <u>skin</u> or <u>breathe in</u> — so many doctors and nurses didn't like or use it.
4) The use of <u>antiseptic</u> conditions reduced death rates from as high as <u>50%</u> to about <u>15%</u>. By <u>1890</u> antiseptics were being used by most European and American surgeons.

J. Lister

Asepsis **reduced the need for** Nasty Chemicals

By going from <u>killing germs</u> to making a <u>germ-free</u> (aseptic) environment, surgeons have been able to avoid using large amounts of <u>antiseptic</u> in the theatre.

The Aseptic Operating Theatre

1) Instruments are carefully <u>sterilised</u> before use, usually with high temperature steam (120°C).
2) Theatre staff <u>sterilise their hands</u> before entering — and wear sterile gowns, masks, gloves and hats. Surgical <u>gloves</u> were invented by <u>William Halsted</u> in <u>1889</u>.
3) The theatres themselves are kept <u>scrupulously clean</u> and fed with <u>sterile air</u>. Special tents can be placed around the operating table to maintain an area of even stricter hygiene in <u>high risk</u> cases.

Make a Lister them facts — then germ up on them...

Right, a couple of tricky words here. The key to the page is to understand the difference between "<u>antiseptic</u>" and "<u>aseptic</u>". Of course you do need to know about the <u>methods</u> used as well. Remember that Lister started using carbolic acid <u>before</u> he'd heard about the germ theory. He was able to <u>improve</u> his methods later when he <u>understood</u> how they worked.

Blood Transfusion, X-rays and Keyhole Surgery

Blood transfusions, radiography and keyhole surgery have revolutionised 20th century medicine.

Karl Landsteiner discovered Blood Groups in 1900

1) Blood circulates rapidly, so it doesn't take long to bleed to death if a major blood vessel is cut. Surgery often causes heavy bleeding.
2) The concept of blood transfusions was known from at least the 17th century, when Jean-Baptiste Denys carried out a cross-species transfusion to a human (1667).
3) The problem was that sometimes it worked and sometimes the blood of the recipient clogged — they died and no-one knew why.
4) Then in 1900, Karl Landsteiner discovered blood groups and the importance of compatibility. He found that certain groups of blood couldn't be mixed together as they would clog the blood vessels.
5) During the First World War sodium citrate was found to stop clotting when blood came into contact with the air. This allowed blood to be stored more easily.
6) In 1946 the British National Blood Transfusion Service was established.

X-rays and Radiography — look before you cut

1) X-rays were discovered by Wilhelm Roentgen in 1895. They pass easily through soft flesh, but less well through bone. They also affect photographic film.
2) These factors allow simple X-ray images to be produced by directing X-rays at a body part in front of a photographic plate.
3) In computerised axial tomography (CAT), a scanner rotates 180° around the body, aiming thin beams of X-rays at receptors on the opposite side of the person. A computer analyses the results and produces an image of a slice of the body. The slices can be built up into a 3D image of the body.
4) Between 1896 and 1898 Antoine Henri Becquerel and Pierre and Marie Curie discovered the first radioactive isotopes. Radioactive isotopes are used:

H. Becquerel

M. Curie

- to treat cancers as part of radiotherapy
- in immunosuppression (see p.67).
- as tracers in diagnosis — mildly radioactive material is swallowed or injected and medics can detect its movement around the body.

Keyhole Surgery is also good for investigating illness

1) Keyhole surgery is a technique (developed in the 1980s) which makes surgery less invasive. It's popular with patients because scars are smaller and recovery is quicker.
2) In keyhole surgery, a surgical instrument called an endoscope is put through a small cut. It gives out light and feeds back a picture to a screen, letting the surgeon see inside the body.
3) Other instruments are needed for the actual surgery, which are introduced through even smaller cuts in the skin. Keyhole surgery is usually performed under a general anaesthetic.
4) This technique is useful for investigating the causes of pain or infertility. It's also used for vasectomies, removing cysts or the appendix, mending hernias and other minor operations.

Blood confusion? — grouping around in the dark...

Don't forget that governments often play key roles in discoveries, e.g. supplying money to fund the research. And government spending is often heavily influenced by social attitudes.

Transplants and Repair

Like keyhole surgery, many other surgical techniques came of age in the last half-century.

Transplants — a brand new branch of surgery

> Replacing worn out body parts is something we're still just beginning to get the hang of. Mechanical parts are quite common now for joint replacement and prosthetic (artificial) limbs, but artificial vital organs cannot compare to the real thing. Transplant surgery using donor organs has usually been the only option.

1) The first organ to be transplanted was the kidney (in 1951), closely followed by the cornea of the eye.

2) Livers, lungs, pancreases and bone marrow are also transplanted, but the organ that has excited most interest has always been the heart. Apart from problems with rejection (which you get with all organ transplants), with heart transplants you also have to:

- keep the body supplied with blood and oxygen
- get the new heart to beat after the operation

In many patients, you also have to deal with additional problems in other parts of the cardiovascular system and other organs.

3) The first heart transplant was carried out by Christiaan Barnard on the 3rd December 1967. The patient only survived for 18 days.

4) The poor life expectancy of patients soon led to a temporary stopping of heart transplants.

5) The major problem for any transplant is rejection, which is when the host body's immune system attacks the implant. The immune system has to be suppressed until the implant is accepted by the body.

Rejection can be cruel.

6) At first corticosteroids were used as immunosuppressants — but they often stopped all resistance to diseases like pneumonia (Christiaan Barnard's first patient died of pneumonia).

7) Cyclosporin was approved for use in 1983 — a fungus-derived drug which has since been used successfully with many patients. A fungus was also the source of tacrolimus (FK506), another immunosuppressant drug approved for use in 1994.

Wars sped the development of Plastic Surgery

1) Skin grafting had been known in Renaissance Europe and since ancient times in India — but infection had limited its usefulness.

2) Harold Gillies began working with burns victims from the First World War.

3) His work was continued during the Second World War by his assistant, Archibald McIndoe — probably the most famous plastic surgeon ever. A lot of McIndoe's patients were pilots who had been trapped inside burning aircraft.

4) McIndoe's unit in East Grinstead took advantage of new developments in antibacterial drugs and surgical techniques. The staff there also worked very hard to help their patients through the psychological effects of their injuries.

Plastic surgery — it's no skin off my nose...

Don't forget advances like these always build on past advances. You might have to compare advances at different times, so it's best to get some practice in now. Think of the similarities and differences — think what factors they had in common. And when you think you know the key bits, turn over the page and scribble them down — then check you've got them all.

Revision Summary for Sections 7-9

That's a dramatic section for you to get to grips with — taking us right up to the present day. All these advances have taken medicine from being a scary last resort that would probably do more harm than good, to being the shining clean and bright marvel it is today. If these sections don't make you want to be a historian, maybe you should think about being a doctor instead. Either way, you'll need to be able to answer these questions without checking back through the section — so keep going through them till you can.

1) Where did the technique of inoculation originate and by what route did it reach Britain?

2) Describe the technique Lady Montagu used to inoculate her patients.

3) What observation led Jenner to try vaccination?

4) In what year was the small pox vaccination made compulsory in England?

5) Give two reasons why some people were opposed to vaccinations.

6) How did Florence Nightingale help the field of nursing?

7) What was the name of Mary Seacole's establishment in the Crimea?

8) Who was the first person to demonstrate that germs caused disease? How did he do this?

9) What was the name of the scientist who discovered the bacteria that cause cholera?

10) Explain how a mistake led to the discovery of the vaccine against chicken cholera.

11) What was Loeffler's theory about how germs cause diseases?

12) Why were antibodies nicknamed 'magic bullets'?

13) In what year did Fleming discover penicillin?

14) What did Domagk discover about the dye prontosil?

15) How did the Second World War help get penicillin into mass production?

16) Give another common name for nitrous oxide.

17) Give two drawbacks of ether as an anaesthetic.

18) Explain the negative effects of the introduction of anaesthetics.

19) What is the difference between antisepsis and asepsis?

20) How did the work of Joseph Lister reduce death rates in surgery?

21) Who invented surgical gloves?

22) Why did blood transfusions often not work when they were first attempted in the 17th and 18th centuries? What discovery helped overcome this problem?

23) In what year was the British National Blood Transfusion Service established?

24) Who discovered X-rays?

25) Give two reasons why keyhole surgery is popular with patients.

26) What was the first organ to be transplanted and in which year?

27) Who carried out the first heart transplant?

28) Why are immunosuppressants used for organ transplants?

29) Which famous plastic surgeon carried out pioneering work in East Grinstead during World War Two?

Childbirth in the Middle Ages

The <u>Middle Ages</u> and <u>Renaissance</u> saw little development of ideas on childbirth.

Midwifery, Obstetrics and Gynaecology — useful words...

1) <u>Midwifery</u> is what a <u>midwife</u> does — it's the branch of <u>nursing</u> that helps with <u>childbirth</u>.
2) <u>Obstetrics</u> is the branch of <u>medicine</u> that covers <u>childbirth</u> — so it includes midwifery.
3) <u>Gynaecology</u> is the branch of medicine that deals with problems specific to <u>women</u>, but <u>not</u> including obstetrics. It covers things like infertility and menstrual problems.

Medieval Arabs and Christians had childbirth specialists

1) The early Islamic Arabs had <u>female doctors</u> who assisted in obstetrics and gynaecology.
2) In the Christian West <u>midwives</u> developed an <u>apprenticeship</u> approach to training, which was completely separate from the training of doctors in the developing <u>universities</u>. There was little connection between the two until the <u>16th century</u>.

The Renaissance saw slow progress

1) <u>Ambroise Paré</u> (1510-1590), who is most famous for his work on gunshot wounds and amputations, also covered pregnancy in a book on surgery — mind you, he did record <u>35 live children</u> from <u>one pregnancy</u>. Eucharius Rösslin wrote the <u>earliest</u> surviving book on <u>midwifery</u> in <u>1513</u>.
2) The French <u>Chamberlens</u> family invented specialised obstetric forceps. They brought them to England when they fled <u>religious persecution</u> in <u>16th century</u> France.
3) Male midwives (<u>accoucheurs</u>) became fashionable amongst the elite in <u>17th century</u> France — the majority of people stuck to the more <u>traditional</u> option of women though.
4) The medical profession became more interested in obstetrics in the <u>18th century</u>, and the first British <u>school of midwifery</u> opened in <u>1725</u>. William Smellie published '<u>The Theory and Practice of Midwifery</u>'. Traditional midwives were <u>sceptical</u> of his writings.

5) Childbirth was a very <u>dangerous activity</u>. Gravestones and registers of deaths during the Renaissance period and onwards show how many women died in their <u>twenties</u> during or soon after pregnancy.
6) There were primitive <u>condoms</u> in the <u>17th century</u> and earlier, but the lack of effective, <u>widely available</u> contraception before the <u>19th century</u> made chastity the only effective <u>family planning</u>.

Learn about childbirth — don't have a midwife crisis...

Notice how <u>midwifery</u> has often been taught and practised completely <u>separately</u> from other areas of medicine. Think about the <u>reasons</u> for this, and how <u>social attitudes</u> have played a part in its development. You need to remember all the <u>key points</u> here — test yourself to make sure.

Population Growth and Family Planning

Big improvements were made from the Industrial Revolution onwards.

Industrial Revolution — mass (re)production

1) The industrial age saw a huge rise in population growth.

2) This was despite the poor conditions in cities, which made women less likely to survive a normal pregnancy. Lack of exercise, pollution-related diseases and deficiency diseases like rickets all weakened people, as did epidemics of smallpox, tuberculosis and cholera.

Giving birth without anaesthetic? We are not amused!

3) Some people raised religious objections to using anaesthetics in childbirth. They thought that a line in the Bible said women were meant to suffer pain during childbirth. These ideas were only really defeated when Queen Victoria asked for chloroform during the birth of Prince Leopold.

4) The development of antiseptics did a lot to reduce the deaths of women following childbirth — especially Semmelweis's use of chloride of lime to control post-natal puerperal fever.

5) Gynaecology as a separate branch of surgery dates from the mid-1800s, with much of the pioneering work being done in America. J.M. Simms opened the first gynaecological hospital in New York in the 1850s.

Family Planning help had to wait till the 20th Century

1) In 1798 Thomas Robert Malthus was the first to suggest that the human species might increase in numbers beyond its ability to feed itself.

2) The reduction of deaths in childbirth meant an increased rate of population growth — and a greater need for family planning.

3) Clinics providing barrier and chemical forms of contraception and family planning advice were pioneered in the 1920s — by Marie Stopes in Britain and Margaret Sanger in America.

4) Contraceptive pills were first available in the early 1960s. For a while the pill and effective antibiotics seemed to offer security from unwanted pregnancy and sexually-transmitted diseases. This helped fuel the sexual revolution of the 1960s. HIV changed that.

5) The World Health Organisation and the UN Population Fund have been working to bring effective family planning to the developing world.

There have been Developments in Infertility Treatments

1) Recently, new infertility treatments have been developed.

2) Most famous is IVF (in vitro fertilisation — or test-tube babies). The external fertilisation of an egg before implantation in the uterus was first done for humans in 1977.

3) Eggs, semen or even embryos can also be frozen and stored for a long time before being allowed to develop into babies. This can be useful — e.g. healthy sperm might be stored before a treatment that could leave a patient infertile.

Children — I give them a wide birth myself...

Queen Victoria's decision to use chloroform was one of those major turning points you need to know about. That's what was needed to change the social and religious attitudes of the day. Communications were also important though — without them, there'd have been no debate, and few people would have known of the Queen's actions — or of chloroform for that matter.

City Slums and Cholera

Medieval and Renaissance towns had <u>failed</u> to reach the standards of public health seen in <u>Roman</u> times — but the <u>Industrial Revolution</u> (which started about 1750) made things even worse.

The Industrial Revolution was bad for your health

1) The towns of the <u>medieval period</u> were not densely packed with rows and rows of buildings as we see them today. Within a town there were <u>gardens</u> for growing <u>vegetables</u> and keeping <u>pigs and chickens</u>. There were also <u>orchards</u> of fruit trees.

2) <u>Industry</u> and changes in agriculture brought more people into the towns. The spaces <u>filled up</u> with <u>factories</u> and <u>poor quality housing</u>. Anyone who owned land could build on it without <u>planning permission</u> — and there were no building standards <u>regulations</u>.

3) People didn't believe the <u>government</u> had the right to tell people what to do with <u>their land</u>. They expected "<u>no-intervention</u>" policies from the government (<u>laissez-faire</u>).

4) Attempts at providing <u>fresh water</u> and <u>removing sewage</u> and <u>rubbish</u> were often <u>inadequate</u>. Sewage was discharged into <u>rivers</u>, overflowing <u>cesspits</u> or even into the <u>street</u>. <u>Smoke</u> from houses and factories filled the air.

5) Diseases like <u>smallpox</u>, <u>influenza</u>, <u>typhus</u> and <u>typhoid fever</u> were common.

Cholera — an epidemic within a year of arrival

1) <u>Cholera</u> reached Britain from the East in <u>1831</u>. It was an <u>epidemic</u> by <u>1832</u>.

2) Cholera spreads when <u>infected sewage</u> gets into <u>drinking water</u>. It causes such extreme <u>diarrhoea</u> that sufferers often die from <u>loss of water</u> and <u>minerals</u>. Both <u>rich</u> and <u>poor</u> people caught the disease.

3) The <u>government</u> started to introduce <u>regulations</u> about the <u>burial</u> of the dead, but the epidemic declined and <u>interest</u> was lost.

4) People did not know what <u>caused</u> cholera. Epidemics <u>recurred</u> in <u>1848</u>, <u>1854</u> and <u>1866</u>.

Chadwick's Report got people thinking

1) In <u>1842</u>, <u>Edwin Chadwick</u> published a '<u>Report on the Sanitary Condition of the Labouring Population of Great Britain</u>'. His revolutionary idea was that <u>improved public health</u> provision and a <u>healthy workforce</u> would <u>save money</u> rather than cost money.

2) The report and statistics describing levels of <u>sickness and mortality</u> shocked some of the <u>privileged classes</u>. People campaigned for improvements and in <u>1844</u> the <u>Health of Towns Association</u> was set up.

3) Responding to calls from the Health of Towns Association, the government introduced a <u>Public Health Bill</u>. It was opposed at first, but was finally passed when a new <u>cholera epidemic</u> broke out. It became the first <u>Public Health Act</u>, in <u>1848</u>.

4) The main provision of the act was for <u>Central and local Health Boards</u>. The local boards had to be <u>approved</u> by ratepayers, and the Central Board lasted until it was <u>dismantled</u> in <u>1854</u>.

Learn the facts — give your brain a clean bill of health...

OK, so basically the Industrial Revolution was a time of very <u>poor living conditions</u> for lots of workers. There were loads of large towns without proper <u>sanitation</u> or <u>clean water</u>. And surprise surprise, there were epidemics. <u>Chadwick's</u> report was a landmark.

The Defeat of Laissez-Faire

John Snow linked cholera to contaminated water, while more voices joined the call for action.

Snow linked Cholera to Contaminated Water

1) The connection between contaminated water and cholera was discovered by John Snow in 1854.
2) He studied the occurrence of a cholera outbreak in the Broad Street area of London and noticed that the victims all used the same water pump. So he removed the handle from the pump — and ended the outbreak.

The 1860s and 70s saw the Defeat of Laissez-Faire

1) Snow was proved right about the spread of disease when Pasteur discovered germs.
2) In 1871 and 1872 the government responded to proposals of the Medical Officer of Health, Sir John Simon. It formed the Local Government Board and divided the country into "sanitary areas" administered by medical officers of health.
3) Another Public Health Act was brought in by Disraeli's government in 1875, along with the Artisans' Dwellings Act. The 1875 Act was more effective than the earlier one because it forced local councils to act on public health.
4) The Artisans' Dwellings Act allowed for compulsory purchase of slum housing and rebuilding by local councils (although the Act was seldom used).

> This Act owed much to the work of Octavia Hill, who was concerned with the terrible conditions in which people were living and so developed a model housing scheme. Hill was also determined that people should have access to green spaces for their health and well-being. She campaigned to save open spaces from being built on and ended up co-founding the National Trust in 1895.

5) Victorian engineering produced improvements in the form of brick-lined sewer networks and steam-driven pumped water systems — such as the Boughton Pumping Station.

But Life in 1900 wasn't much Better

1) Slums were still a feature of big cities and industrial towns at the start of the 20th century.
2) Poor people were often housed in tenements — these were damp, insanitary and had no running water. Large families lived together in one room and shared a toilet with their neighbours.
3) The poor worked long hours for low wages. Many people couldn't afford to see a doctor when they were sick or provide their children with three decent meals a day.
4) There were 140 infant deaths for every 1000 births, today it's less than 5.
5) Patent medicines continued to be popular. They had secret recipes and were sold with extravagant claims, but they often did more harm than good.

Children in a London slum, c. 1900

Snow use ignoring them — those germs won't go away...

We take it for granted now that the government gets involved in public health. But not so long ago that just wasn't the case. It took a big change in people's beliefs for that to happen.

Philanthropists and Liberal Reforms

The Liberal government elected in 1906 made many important changes.

Philanthropists were rich people who Helped the poor

1) In 1889, the shipping owner Charles Booth surveyed living conditions in London's East End and published 'Life and Labour of the People in London' — it showed a clear link between poverty and ill health.
2) A similar survey was made in York by Seebohm Rowntree, a member of the family that made Rowntree's chocolate. His work, published in 1901, would go on to heavily influence the policies of the Liberal Chancellor David Lloyd George.
3) The other famous chocolate makers, the Cadburys, tried to provide quality homes and improve lifestyles for workers at their factory in Bournville, near Birmingham. Titus Salt did a similar thing in Saltaire (c.1850) in Yorkshire.
4) These philanthropist businessmen were great examples of how to make money and treat your workers well.
5) When the Boer War broke out in 1899, army officers found that 40% of volunteers were unfit for military service — mostly due to poverty-related illnesses linked with poor diet and living conditions. Similar problems were encountered during the First World War. Britain, like the Romans, realised it needed a healthy population to have an efficient army.
6) Many workers organised Friendly Societies, which were often linked to trade unions. Workers paid a subscription each week and in return received medical help and other benefits.

Liberal Government Reforms — Social Security measures

1) By 1906 the link between poverty and ill health had been well and truly established. The newly-elected Liberal government realised it had to take action. Many MPs were especially worried about losing votes to the relatively new Labour Party — which promised to look after interests of the working classes.
2) So — under the guidance of Lloyd George* — the Liberals started to introduce measures that are still important to our social security today:

David Lloyd George

- Free school meals — 1906,
- School medical inspections — 1907,
- Old Age Pension Act — 1909,
- Labour Exchanges (Job Centres) — 1909,
- National Insurance Act — 1911.

* David Lloyd George was Chancellor of the Exchequer at the time of the reforms. He became Prime Minister in 1916.

3) Lloyd George had to overcome a lot of opposition from the House of Lords to get many of these reforms through.
4) National Insurance wasn't compulsory and it only covered people who paid in. These people could then get sick pay and medical treatment from a panel doctor working for the scheme. The scheme also provided unemployment pay.
5) The reforms weren't perfect, but they marked the start of the modern welfare state.

David Lloyd George — so good they named him thrice...

All those schemes at the bottom of the page are really important. Make sure you understand just how big a breakthrough they were. Also, don't forget there was plenty of opposition — people argued that governments shouldn't interfere in people's lives.

The Medical Profession and Women

Women struggled for a long time to be accepted as qualified doctors.

Women had to fight to re-enter the Medical Profession

1) Women were not allowed to attend universities in the early 19th century. As a result, they couldn't qualify as doctors. Many Victorian men regarded women as being less able to work in jobs requiring professionalism, intelligence or lack of squeamishness.

2) It's likely that the first British woman to qualify as a doctor had to pretend to be a man. Margaret Ann Bulkley was born some time in the 1790s. She's thought to have trained at Edinburgh University as "James Barry". After qualifying in 1812, she joined the army in time to serve at the Battle of Waterloo and was eventually promoted to Assistant Surgeon. She served in the army for 46 years and was only found out when she died in 1865.

Margaret was the first to admit her disguise needed work.

3) Elizabeth Blackwell (an English-born American) was the first woman in modern times to be awarded a medical degree in her own name from a western training college (1849).

4) The first British women to practise openly as qualified modern doctors both had to train privately or abroad. Their names were Elizabeth Garrett Anderson and Sophia Jex-Blake.

- Garrett Anderson was trained privately before being accepted as a qualified doctor by the Society of Apothecaries in 1865. She used the society's rules to force it to recognise her — but afterwards they changed their rules to stop other women doing the same. She was awarded a medical degree by the University of Paris in 1870.
- Sophia Jex-Blake gained entry to Edinburgh University, but was refused a degree when her entry was declared unlawful. She then co-founded the London School of Medicine for Women in 1874, and gained her own qualification from the University of Bern.

More Women are now qualifying as doctors

1) The need for women in professional roles increased during the world wars (1914-1918 and 1939-1945).

2) The 1975 Sex Discrimination Act meant that equal opportunities for men and women had to be available in all jobs.

3) Today around 45% of doctors are women and female GPs could soon outnumber their male counterparts.

4) Women are still under-represented at the top level though — they make up only 28% of consultants.

The lengths some people go to get an education...

You need to think about what factors held women back and which ones allowed them to succeed. You also need to remember that people like Garrett Anderson were instrumental in getting women accepted as doctors. As usual, learn the stuff, turn the page, then scribble it down.

The National Health Service

The setting up of the <u>NHS</u> in 1948 was a great achievement of the post-war government.

There were Economic and Social Problems 1918-1939

1) After the First World War, Lloyd George promised to make Britain a land "<u>fit for heroes</u>". A <u>Ministry of Health</u> was set up in <u>1919</u>, and grants were given to build <u>council houses</u>.
2) But the First World War had <u>drained Britain's resources</u>. An economic slump in the 1920s caused <u>rising unemployment</u>. The government <u>cut back spending</u> on welfare.
3) During the <u>1930s</u>, things got worse when there was a <u>global economic depression</u>. By 1932, 22% of British workers were unemployed. Poverty and unemployment were particularly bad in <u>Wales</u>, <u>Scotland</u> and the <u>North of England</u>.
4) Homes in poor areas often had no electricity or sanitation. The <u>1930 Housing Act</u> planned to clear <u>slum housing</u>. Progress was <u>slowed down</u> by the <u>depression</u>.

The Second World War led to pressure for Social Change

1) The <u>Second World War (1939-1945)</u> broke down <u>social distinctions</u> and brought people together whose lives had been very <u>separate</u>. The raising of <u>mass armies</u> made powerful people take notice of the <u>health problems</u> of the poor. Also the <u>evacuation of children</u> increased awareness in rural middle England of how disadvantaged many people were.
2) Air raids, especially the Blitz of <u>1940</u>, prompted the government to set up the <u>Emergency Medical Service</u>. This provided a <u>centralised control</u> of medical services and offered <u>free treatment</u> to air raid casualties. It proved <u>successful</u> under great pressure.
3) After the Second World War people looked for <u>improvements</u> in society. Such feelings led to the <u>1945</u> victory for the <u>Labour Party</u>.

After the Beveridge Report, Bevan introduced the NHS

1) Sir William Beveridge published his famous <u>Beveridge Report</u> in <u>1942</u>. In it he called for the state provision of social security "<u>from the cradle to the grave</u>".
2) The report became a bestseller. In it Beveridge argued that all people should have the <u>right</u> to be free from <u>want</u>, <u>disease</u>, <u>ignorance</u>, <u>squalor</u> and <u>idleness</u>. He called these the five "giants".

The Beverage Report

3) <u>Aneurin Bevan</u> was the Labour Minister for Health who introduced the <u>National Health Service</u>.
4) <u>Compulsory</u> National Insurance was introduced in <u>1948</u> to pay for the NHS. <u>Doctors and dentists</u> were wooed with a <u>fixed payment</u> for each registered patient. They were also allowed to continue treating <u>private</u> fee-paying patients.
5) By <u>1948</u> nearly all hospitals had joined the NHS and <u>92%</u> of doctors had.

A big step forward for the sick...

OK, it's NHS time. It tends to get taken for granted these days, but you've got to remember it hasn't been around that long. It was a major <u>turning point</u>, so make sure you know the factors that led to its formation, and why they were important. Start with these — the <u>Liberal Government</u> 1906-14 (p.73), <u>social attitudes</u>, the <u>Beveridge</u> report, the <u>Labour victory</u> and the <u>war</u>.

The NHS and the WHO

The NHS is now a <u>huge organisation</u>, which employs over <u>one million people</u>.

Millions of people have Benefited from the NHS...

1) The development of <u>ante-</u> and <u>post-natal units</u> with specialist doctors and nurses has <u>reduced the risk</u> of both infant and maternal <u>mortality</u>.
2) Life expectancy for women in England and Wales has risen from <u>70 in 1948</u> to <u>82</u> in 2008.
3) A whole programme of <u>free childhood vaccinations</u> has been introduced — from the <u>BCG</u> (against tuberculosis) in 1948, to <u>measles, mumps and rubella</u> in 1988.
4) Between <u>June 2008</u> and <u>May 2009</u> over <u>16 million</u> people were treated as inpatients by the NHS. A further <u>75 million</u> attended outpatient appointments.
5) The NHS provides <u>free</u> ambulances, accident and emergency care, major surgery, chemotherapy, physiotherapy, health visitors <u>and more</u>.

... but it has had a few Problems

1) Right from the <u>start</u> the demand for <u>NHS</u> services was <u>greater</u> than expected. In <u>1950</u> spending was about <u>£350 million</u> — <u>twice</u> the original budget. Today it runs at over <u>£3500 million</u>.
2) Successive governments have <u>reduced</u> how much of the NHS is <u>free</u> — charges have been reintroduced for things like prescriptions and dental checkups. <u>Aneurin Bevan resigned</u> over prescription charges. <u>Long waiting lists</u> and doubts about the quality of treatment have led many to take out <u>private health insurance</u>, or pay for treatment <u>outside</u> the NHS.
3) Even successes sometimes have their downsides — <u>longer life expectancies</u> have meant more need for care of the <u>elderly</u> and increased costs for the NHS.

Health for the Global Village

1) The <u>World Health Organisation</u> (<u>WHO</u>) was set up in <u>1948</u> as part of the <u>United Nations</u>. It has been very successful in increasing the number of children <u>vaccinated</u> worldwide.
2) Its other major success was the total <u>eradication</u> of <u>smallpox</u>. It also works hard trying to eliminate <u>polio</u>, <u>malaria</u> and <u>tuberculosis</u>.

Doctor Doctor — will you be giving me that for free?

The NHS has been <u>heavily criticised</u> in recent years and has certainly had its fair share of <u>problems</u> — many of which are related to <u>rising costs</u>. But it still provides treatment which is "<u>free at the point of delivery</u>" to millions of people in the UK every year. Make sure you know about the NHS's <u>plus points</u> as well as its <u>minuses</u>.

DNA and Genetics

Many recent advances have been based on <u>genetics</u> — so you'd best learn a bit about it.

DNA and Genetics — a continuing development

J.Watson + F.Crick

1) The understanding of inheritance has been a slow development going back into <u>prehistory</u> — to whenever someone noticed that children looked a bit like their parents and could <u>inherit</u> characteristics from them.

2) <u>DNA</u> (deoxyribonucleic acid) is the substance in cell nuclei that contains all our <u>genes</u>. These are the chemical 'instructions' that <u>plan out</u> human characteristics. Your sex, hair colour and the colour of your eyes among billions of other things are all determined by your DNA, which is a <u>mix</u> of <u>your parents' DNA</u>.

3) The structure of <u>DNA</u> was first described in <u>1953</u> by <u>Francis Crick</u> and <u>James Watson</u>. They relied heavily on the work of <u>Rosalind Franklin</u> and <u>Maurice Wilkins</u>. All except <u>Franklin</u> shared in the <u>1962</u> <u>Nobel Prize</u> for Physiology or Medicine. Franklin had <u>died</u> four years earlier in <u>1958</u>.

4) The structure of <u>DNA</u> is a double helix (a kind of spiral) which can reproduce itself by splitting.

5) The <u>Human Genome Project</u> has <u>identified</u> all the genes in <u>human DNA</u>. The task was huge as there are between <u>20 000</u> and <u>25 000 genes</u>. Scientists are now in the process of analysing the results.

Since <u>prehistory</u>, humans have tried to change the characteristics of animals in the form of <u>selective breeding</u>. This has now accelerated as scientists have learnt to <u>manipulate</u> <u>individual genes</u> and <u>splice</u> different genes together to give genetically modified organisms (<u>GMOs</u>) — this is known as <u>genetic engineering</u>. Many people worry about the <u>safety and ethics</u> of this research as it may have unintended consequences and once modified DNA gets out into nature it may be impossible to contain it.

Genetic Conditions — the search for a solution goes on

1) Some conditions such as <u>cystic fibrosis</u>, <u>haemophilia</u> and <u>sickle-cell anaemia</u> are <u>genetic</u> — they can be passed on from one generation to the next.

2) In recent years, <u>research</u> into genetic conditions has <u>increased</u>. Now that scientists have <u>identified</u> the genes responsible for certain conditions, they can:

- <u>Test</u> for certain genetic conditions <u>in the womb</u> (e.g. Down's syndrome) or <u>soon after birth</u> (e.g. PKU and hypothyroidism). An early diagnosis can make treatment <u>more effective</u>.
- Produce — in some cases — a <u>synthetic protein</u> to replicate the work of the faulty gene. E.g. Hurler syndrome can be <u>treated</u> using the synthetic <u>enzyme</u> laronidase.

3) Scientists are now looking at <u>curing</u> inherited conditions using techniques such as <u>gene therapy</u>, which tries to replace disease-causing genes with good ones.

The Human Gnome Project — it might improve our elf...

The <u>structure of DNA</u> was probably one of the most important discoveries of the past 50 years — it led to the sequencing of the entire human genome and the discovery of the genes behind many <u>genetic conditions</u>. Now doctors can <u>diagnose</u> (and in some cases <u>treat</u>) these conditions <u>more effectively</u>. In the future, it may even be possible to <u>cure</u> them.

Technology and Industry

Developments in <u>science and technology</u> have contributed to <u>advances</u> in medicine.

The Pharmaceutical Industry has really taken off

1) In the <u>late 1800s</u> the <u>chemical industry</u> in places like Germany and Switzerland was <u>booming</u>. This lead to the growth of the modern <u>pharmaceutical industry</u>.
2) For the first time, it was possible to manufacture <u>drugs and medicines</u> on a <u>large scale</u>, and make them available to <u>lots of people</u>.
3) The late-19th and 20th centuries saw the discovery and <u>mass production</u> of <u>aspirin</u> (1899), <u>insulin</u> (1921), <u>sulphonamides</u> (1932) and <u>more</u>.
4) <u>Penicillin</u> was first produced <u>commercially</u> by American pharmaceutical firms during the <u>Second World War</u>. It helped to save the lives of countless Allied soldiers (see p.63).
5) <u>Antibiotics</u> are still used today to treat a <u>huge range</u> of <u>bacterial infections</u>.
6) The pharmaceutical industry has also made <u>widespread vaccination</u> possible. As a result of vaccination programmes beginning in the <u>1950s</u>, the disease <u>polio</u> has nearly been <u>eradicated</u>. More recent vaccinations to become available include those against <u>meningitis C</u> and the <u>HPV virus</u> (which causes cervical cancer).
7) After the <u>thalidomide tragedy</u> (see p.79) many countries passed laws which introduced <u>more stringent testing</u> for new medicines.

Advances in Communication have helped Research

1) Many of the medical advances over the course of the last century have been made possible by <u>improvements</u> in <u>communication technology</u>.
2) Scientists from all over the world are able to share their <u>ideas</u> and <u>findings</u> by <u>phone</u>, <u>email</u> and the <u>internet</u>. <u>Long-distance travel</u> has also become <u>cheaper</u> and <u>easier</u> — allowing researchers to attend <u>international</u> seminars and conferences.
3) <u>Government-funded research</u> tends to get <u>shared</u> more. Companies tend to keep research <u>secret</u> so that they can <u>patent</u> new treatments. On the other hand, few new medicines would be developed if there wasn't any <u>profit</u> in it — the research process is hugely <u>expensive</u>.

Advances in Technology have helped Diagnostics

Developments in technology mean doctors can more <u>accurately</u> diagnose and treat conditions.

1) <u>Medical imaging</u> using sound waves (<u>ultrasound</u>) enables doctors to build up a picture of what's happening <u>inside</u> the body. This technique was first developed around <u>50 years ago</u>.
2) A more recent development is the <u>MRI scanner</u> (<u>1973</u>), which uses <u>radio waves</u> and <u>magnets</u> to visualise the internal structures of the body.
3) The use of <u>fibre-optic cables</u> inside an <u>endoscope</u> allows doctors to look inside the body, e.g. through a small cut in the skin or down the patient's airways. During <u>keyhole surgery</u> (see p.66), endoscopes containing small instruments are used to operate on the patient.

Technology is also helping people to monitor their <u>own health</u>. Products like <u>pregnancy testing kits</u> and devices to monitor <u>blood sugar levels</u> are now available from pharmacies.

Communication — important in research and relationships

Lots of <u>science and technology</u> here, that's for sure. But don't forget there are many other relevant factors. Take <u>communications</u> and <u>governments</u>. Without governments providing lots of <u>cash</u>, a lot of important scientific research wouldn't get done — especially research where any applications might be a long way in the future.

Modern Healthcare

Modern healthcare faces a whole <u>new set of challenges</u> to those 100 years ago...

HIV *and* AIDS — *health problems in the new century*

1) <u>HIV</u> (Human Immunodeficiency Virus) is thought to have originated in <u>Africa</u>, but the disease it causes (<u>AIDS</u> — Acquired Immune Deficiency Syndrome) was first identified in <u>America</u> in <u>1981</u>.
2) In <u>2007</u>, around <u>33 million</u> people worldwide were thought to be infected with the HIV virus. <u>Two-thirds</u> of those live in sub-Saharan Africa.
3) Drugs such as <u>antiretrovirals</u> can be used to treat people with HIV. Antiretrovirals block the virus from replicating and so <u>slow down</u> the progression into AIDS. They can be very effective, but they're also <u>expensive</u> — a major <u>problem</u> in <u>developing countries</u>.
4) The <u>WHO</u> is coordinating efforts to look for <u>vaccines and cures</u>, but neither is available yet.
5) Better <u>health promotion</u>, <u>sex education</u> and <u>free condoms</u> can all help to reduce the spread of infection.

High-Tech *medicine has its own Problems*

1) <u>Not</u> all the developments in modern medicine have turned out <u>well</u>:

- <u>Overuse</u> of <u>antibiotics</u> is leading to the evolution of <u>superbugs</u> (like <u>MRSA</u>) which are resistant to our antibacterial drugs.
- The drug <u>thalidomide</u> was used in the <u>1960s</u> to treat <u>morning sickness</u> in pregnant women — many babies were born with under-developed limbs as a result.

2) Mistrust of modern medicine and technology has led some people to consider treatment using <u>alternative therapies</u>, e.g. <u>acupuncture</u>, <u>homeopathy</u> and <u>herbal remedies</u>.
3) Mainstream doctors have expressed <u>concern</u> about alternative medicine, believing that it might do more harm than good. However, some medical practitioners are now working with alternative therapists to see if a <u>complementary approach</u> will result in benefits to the patient.

The Roles of Doctors and Nurses have Changed

1) Over the course of the last century, medicine has <u>changed a lot</u>. In 1900, there were <u>very few drugs available</u> for doctors to prescribe their patients and even less <u>specialist diagnostic equipment</u> for them to use — for this reason people were usually seen <u>at home</u>. Doctors now treat the majority of their patients in <u>clinics</u>.
2) <u>Training</u> has had to become <u>better regulated</u>.
   - Since <u>1919</u>, nurses have had to be <u>registered</u> — and have a <u>full nursing qualification</u>.
   - All medical professionals have to regularly update their skills by attending training courses. This is called <u>Continuous Professional Development (CPD)</u> and was introduced in <u>2001</u>.
3) Advances in <u>medical technology</u> allow many people to take some <u>control</u> over their own treatment. Things like cheap <u>blood pressure monitors</u> mean that patients can often monitor their conditions <u>at home</u>.

Modern medicine — and the prognosis is... good?

Phew, some heavy stuff to finish up with, I'm afraid. This sort of thing crops up in the news a lot, so it's pretty hard to avoid some of it. You might not be able to avoid it in the <u>exams</u> either, so it's as well to learn it. It's the kind of thing it's probably a <u>good idea</u> to know about anyway. As usual, when you think you know it, <u>turn the page</u> and <u>scribble</u> it all down. Then <u>check</u> you know it.

Revision Summary for Sections 10-11

At last, the end of our journey through the history of medicine. Except for these questions, of course. So you haven't finished yet. In fact you haven't finished until you've passed those exams — and until then you need to go over this stuff loads. Until it's all sunk in in fact.

1) What is obstetrics?

2) How did the training of doctors and midwives differ before the 16th century?

3) What did the Chamberlens family invent?

4) Who was the author of 'The Theory and Practice of Midwifery'?

5) Describe one development that occurred during the Industrial Revolution which reduced the numbers of women who died following childbirth.

6) What was Thomas Malthus's theory?

7) What were the names of the women who set up family planning clinics in Britain and in the US?

8) What does IVF stand for?

9) In what year did cholera reach Britain?

10) When was the first Public Health Act passed? What was its main provision?

11) How did John Snow stop the cholera outbreak in the Broad Street area of London?

12) a) What factors lead to the Liberal reforms in 1906?
    b) What were the main innovations of these reforms?

13) a) Why were Victorian men reluctant to allow female doctors?
    b) Who were the first two British women to train openly as doctors?

14) How did the Blitz of 1940 help change attitudes towards the provision of publicly-funded health services?

15) What was the name of the Minister for Health who introduced the National Health Service?

16) Name two things that the NHS now charges for that it didn't when it was created.

17) a) What does WHO stand for?
    b) What have been the WHO's major successes?

18) Discuss the importance of the work carried out on the structure of DNA to modern medicine.

19) How has the ability to produce drugs on a large scale helped the fight against disease?

20) How have improvements in communication technology helped medical research?

21) Outline one reason why some people are now turning to alternative therapies for treatment.

22) How have the roles of doctors and nurses changed since 1900?

Important Dates

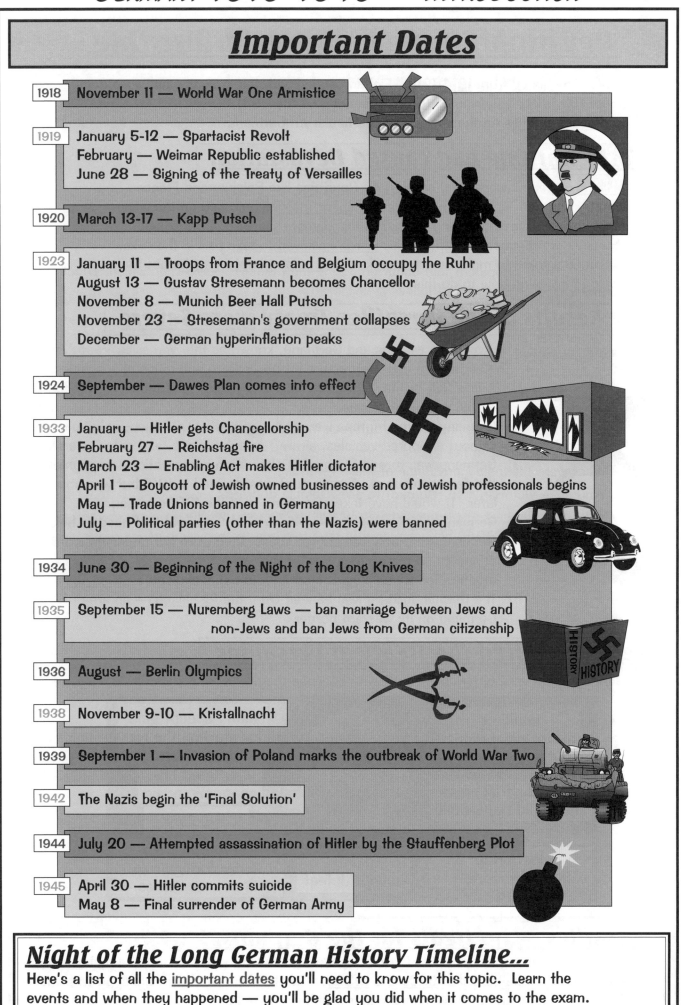

1918 | November 11 — World War One Armistice

1919 | January 5-12 — Spartacist Revolt
February — Weimar Republic established
June 28 — Signing of the Treaty of Versailles

1920 | March 13-17 — Kapp Putsch

1923 | January 11 — Troops from France and Belgium occupy the Ruhr
August 13 — Gustav Stresemann becomes Chancellor
November 8 — Munich Beer Hall Putsch
November 23 — Stresemann's government collapses
December — German hyperinflation peaks

1924 | September — Dawes Plan comes into effect

1933 | January — Hitler gets Chancellorship
February 27 — Reichstag fire
March 23 — Enabling Act makes Hitler dictator
April 1 — Boycott of Jewish owned businesses and of Jewish professionals begins
May — Trade Unions banned in Germany
July — Political parties (other than the Nazis) were banned

1934 | June 30 — Beginning of the Night of the Long Knives

1935 | September 15 — Nuremberg Laws — ban marriage between Jews and
non-Jews and ban Jews from German citizenship

1936 | August — Berlin Olympics

1938 | November 9-10 — Kristallnacht

1939 | September 1 — Invasion of Poland marks the outbreak of World War Two

1942 | The Nazis begin the 'Final Solution'

1944 | July 20 — Attempted assassination of Hitler by the Stauffenberg Plot

1945 | April 30 — Hitler commits suicide
May 8 — Final surrender of German Army

Night of the Long German History Timeline...

Here's a list of all the <u>important dates</u> you'll need to know for this topic. Learn the
events and when they happened — you'll be glad you did when it comes to the exam.

The Aftermath of World War One

World War One lasted from 1914-1918. Fighting ended with the armistice on November 11th 1918. The winners (Britain, France and the USA) then imposed peace treaties on the losers — in particular on Germany.

World War One had caused Devastation

1) Millions of people were dead or injured. Countries like Belgium and France were devastated — the main powers had spent too much money on the war.
2) Many people wanted Germany to take all the blame, especially in Britain and France — so Germany and their allies weren't allowed to take part in the talks.
3) Everyone wanted to make sure a war like this wouldn't happen again, but they couldn't agree on how to do this.

The Results of the Versailles Treaty were Severe

The peace settlement between the winners and Germany, known as the 'Versailles Treaty', was signed in June 1919. The settlement cost Germany a lot of territory and much else besides.

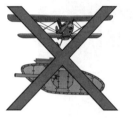

1) Article 231 of the treaty said Germany had to take the blame for the war — the War-Guilt Clause.
2) Germany's armed forces were reduced to 100 000 men, only volunteers, without armoured vehicles, aircraft or submarines, and only 6 warships.
3) Germany was forced to pay £6600 million in reparations — payments for the damage caused. The amount was decided in 1921 but was changed later. It would have taken Germany until the 1980s to pay.
4) Germany lost its empire — areas around the world that used to belong to Germany were now called mandates. They were put under the control of countries on the winning side of the war by the League of Nations — an organisation which aimed to settle international disputes peacefully.
5) The German military was banned from the Rhineland — an area of Germany on its western border.

Germany Hated the Treaty of Versailles

The Germans were very bitter about the treaty because they...

couldn't afford reparations

didn't accept guilt for starting the war

lost industrial areas and could not rebuild

suffered an economic crisis

lost colonies

lost pride without armed forces

didn't accept defeat

often now lived under foreign rule in new countries

Versailles — no treats for the Germans...

This treaty was the key document in Europe for the next twenty years — it had a major impact on world events throughout the 1920s and 1930s. The Germans were very unhappy with the results of the treaty, and it would cause major problems there later...

The Weimar Republic

At the end of the war, Germany got a new <u>democratic</u> system of government.

A New Government Took Over When the Kaiser Abdicated

1) <u>Kaiser Wilhelm II</u> had ruled the German Empire as a <u>monarch</u>. At the end of the First World War there was a period of <u>violent unrest</u> in Germany — and the Kaiser was forced to abdicate in November 1918.

2) In early 1919, a <u>new government</u> took power led by <u>Friedrich Ebert</u> — it changed Germany into a <u>republic</u>. It was set up in <u>Weimar</u>, because there was violence in Berlin. <u>Ebert</u> became the first President, with <u>Scheidemann</u> as Chancellor.

3) Ebert was leader of the <u>Social Democratic Party</u>, a moderate party of socialists. The new government was <u>democratic</u> — they believed the people should say how the country was run.

4) The new German government <u>wasn't invited</u> to the peace conference in 1919 — and had <u>no say</u> in the <u>Versailles Treaty</u>. At first, Ebert <u>refused</u> to sign the treaty, but in the end he had little choice — Germany was too <u>weak</u> to risk restarting the conflict.

The Weimar Constitution made Germany a Republic

THE WEIMAR GOVERNMENT

REICHSRAT
(Upper house could delay measures passed by Reichstag)

REICHSTAG
The new German parliament (elected by proportional representation)

PRESIDENT
Elected every 7 years. Head of army. Chooses the Chancellor.

Friedrich Ebert

<u>Proportional representation</u> is where the number of <u>seats</u> a party wins in parliament is worked out as a <u>proportion</u> of the number of <u>votes</u> they win. This was the system in Germany and it often led to <u>lots</u> of political parties in the Reichstag (German parliament) — making it <u>harder</u> to get laws passed.

The Weimar Republic had Many Problems

1) It was <u>difficult</u> to make decisions because there were so <u>many parties</u> in the Reichstag.

2) It was hard to pick a Chancellor who had the <u>support</u> of most of the Reichstag.

3) The new government had to <u>accept</u> the Versailles Treaty, so they were <u>hated</u> by many Germans because of the loss of territory, the 'war guilt' clause, the reparations etc. (see p.82).

4) There were many outbreaks of <u>trouble</u>, and Ebert agreed to form the <u>Freikorps</u>, a body of soldiers to keep the peace.

Weimar — not a kind of sausage...

The <u>Weimar Republic</u> was set up in a time of <u>defeat</u> — which made it unpopular right from the start. Don't forget — many German people <u>didn't accept</u> the peace settlements at the end of the First World War. Scribble a quick paragraph on the Weimar Republic and how it was set up.

Years of Unrest — 1919-1923

Germany faced all sorts of <u>problems</u> in the years following the First World War.

Reasons for Discontent

1) Thousands of people were <u>poor</u> and <u>starving</u>. An <u>influenza</u> epidemic had killed thousands.
2) Many Germans <u>denied</u> they had lost the war and blamed the '<u>November Criminals</u>' who had agreed to the Armistice and the Treaty of Versailles.
3) Others <u>blamed</u> for losing the war included the communists, the government and the Jews.
4) The government was seen as <u>weak</u> and <u>ineffective</u> — the <u>Treaty of Versailles</u> had made living conditions <u>worse</u> in Germany.

Soon there were Riots and Rebellions

1) In 1919, the <u>communists</u> led by Karl Liebknecht and Rosa Luxemburg tried to <u>take over</u> Berlin in the <u>Spartacist Revolt</u> — but they were defeated by the Freikorps.

Wolfgang Kapp

2) In 1920, some of the right-wing Freikorps themselves took part in the Kapp Putsch (Putsch means revolt) — led by Wolfgang Kapp, they <u>took over</u> Berlin to form another government. The workers staged a General Strike — Kapp <u>gave up</u>. The government <u>didn't</u> punish the rebels, because many judges <u>sympathised</u> with people like Kapp.

3) In 1922 Walter Rathenau was <u>assassinated</u> by former Freikorp members — he'd been Foreign Minister and was <u>Jewish</u>. Many Germans were now anti-Jewish (<u>anti-Semitic</u>).

In 1923 Germany Couldn't Pay the Reparations

France and Belgium occupied the Ruhr — the <u>richest</u> industrial part of Germany — to <u>take resources</u> instead. This led to fury in Germany, while workers in the Ruhr <u>refused</u> to work. German industry was devastated again, plunging the economy into <u>hyperinflation</u>.

1918	Aug 1923	Nov 1923
1/4 Mark	5000 Marks	80 million Marks

HYPERINFLATION - THE PRICE OF AN EGG IN GERMANY

<u>Hyperinflation</u> happens when production can't keep up with the amount of money there is, so the money keeps <u>losing its value</u>.

Hyperinflation had Three Major Results

1) <u>Wages</u> were paid <u>twice a day</u> before prices went up again.
2) The middle classes lost out as <u>bank savings</u> became <u>worthless</u>.
3) The German <u>Mark</u> became <u>worthless</u>.

Hyperinflation — sounds good for blowing up balloons...

Remember that discontent in Germany got <u>worse</u> when the economy <u>went wrong</u> — but there were lots of other factors too. Scribble a list of <u>reasons</u> why there was so much discontent.

Stresemann and Recovery

In August 1923 Stresemann became Chancellor — he gradually led Germany back to recovery.

Stresemann _wanted_ International Cooperation

Stresemann was Chancellor for a few months, then Foreign Minister. He believed Germany's best chance for recovery came from working with other countries.

1) In September 1923 he told the workers in the Ruhr to return to work.
2) He accepted the Dawes Plan in 1924, and introduced a new German Mark called the Rentenmark to make the currency more stable.
3) In 1925 the French and Belgian troops left the Ruhr.
4) In October 1925 he agreed to the Locarno Treaty where the western borders of Germany were agreed, but not the eastern. He won the Nobel Peace Prize for his efforts in this field.
5) In 1926, Germany joined the League of Nations, and became one of the permanent members of the Council.
6) In 1928, Germany was one of 65 countries to sign the Kellogg-Briand Pact. They promised not to use violence to settle disputes.
7) In 1929, the Young Plan replaced the Dawes Plan — reparations would be reduced by three-quarters of the amount, and Germany was given 59 years to pay them.
8) Some big industries (like coal, iron and steel) began to recover, providing jobs and improving the economy. However, some sectors of society remained poor, e.g. peasant farmers.

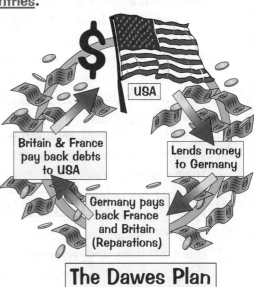

The Dawes Plan

Germany had Begun to Recover — but Depended on US Money

Gustav Stresemann

Life was beginning to look better for Germany thanks to the work of Stresemann. But he died in October 1929, just before the disaster of the Wall Street Crash — a massive stock market crash in the USA which started a global economic depression. The plans he had agreed would only work if the USA had enough money to keep lending to Germany — but now it didn't. Things were suddenly going to get worse again.

The Weimar Republic had many Cultural Achievements

1) Germany's capital Berlin became a centre for culture under the Weimar Republic.
2) There were advances in art, architecture, music and literature. German films were successful — e.g. 'Metropolis' directed by Fritz Lang.
3) Some developments were bold and new, like the drama of Bertholt Brecht. The Bauhaus School of design was highly influential.
4) The Weimar Republic encouraged new ways of critical thinking at places like Frankfurt University.
5) Not everyone approved of these cultural changes — the cabaret culture in Berlin was seen as immoral by some. The culture of the Weimar Republic didn't survive under the Nazis...

It was nearly all okay...

The 1920s were a tough decade in Germany, but Stresemann seemed to have the problems sorted. Scribble a paragraph on the work of Stresemann — his policies at home and abroad.

The Roots of the Nazi Party

The Nazi Party was a small organisation in the 1920s — but it had big ambitions...

Adolf Hitler was the Nazi Leader

1) Born in Austria in 1889, Hitler had lived in Germany from 1912 onwards.
2) He'd been a brave soldier on the Western Front in World War I, winning the Iron Cross twice. He couldn't accept that Germany had lost the war.
3) In 1919, he joined the German Workers' Party, led by Anton Drexler. It was a tiny party — Hitler was the 55th member. In 1920 the name was changed to the National Socialist German Workers' Party (Nazis).
4) Hitler was a charismatic speaker and attracted new members. He took over the leadership of the party.
5) The party set up its own armed group called the SA (or Sturmabteilung) — brown-shirted stormtroopers who protected Nazi leaders and harassed their opponents.

Hitler tried to Overthrow the Government in the Munich Putsch

1) In 1923, things were going badly for the Weimar Republic — it seemed weak.
2) Hitler planned to overthrow the Weimar government — starting by taking control of the government in a region called Bavaria.
3) Hitler's soldiers occupied a beer hall in the Bavarian city of Munich where local government leaders were meeting. He announced that the revolution had begun.
4) The next day Hitler marched into Munich supported by stormtroopers. But the revolt quickly collapsed when police fired on the rebels.

Hitler wrote the book 'Mein Kampf' in Prison

1) Hitler was imprisoned for his role in the Munich Putsch.
2) He wrote a book in prison describing his beliefs and ambitions. The title 'Mein Kampf' means 'My Struggle'.

Believed the ARYANS were a MASTER RACE
(He meant Northern European people, but got it wrong)

Would join Austria and Germany (Anschluss)

Would reverse Versailles Treaty

Would create a greater Germany

ADOLF HITLER MEIN KAMPF

Germans had a right to LEBENSRAUM (more space to live)

He believed other races were inferior

After the Munich Putsch Hitler Changed Tactics

1) The Nazi party was banned after the Munich Putsch. After Hitler was released from prison, he re-established the party with himself as supreme leader.
2) By the mid-1920s, the German economy was starting to recover under Stresemann. As a result, general support for the Nazis declined and overturning the government through a coup no longer seemed realistic.
3) Hitler changed tactics — he now tried to gain control through the democratic system. The Nazi party network was extended nationally, instead of it being a regional party. Propaganda was used to promote the party's beliefs.

The Nazis — ready to sweep to power...

Very few people supported the Nazis at this stage. There were less than 30 000 members by 1925, and in the 1928 elections the Nazis had 12 Reichstag members, compared with 54 communists and 153 Social Democrats. All that was about to change though...

The Rise of the Nazis

The popularity of the Nazi Party <u>soared</u> as a result of the Depression.

The Great Depression caused Poverty and Suffering

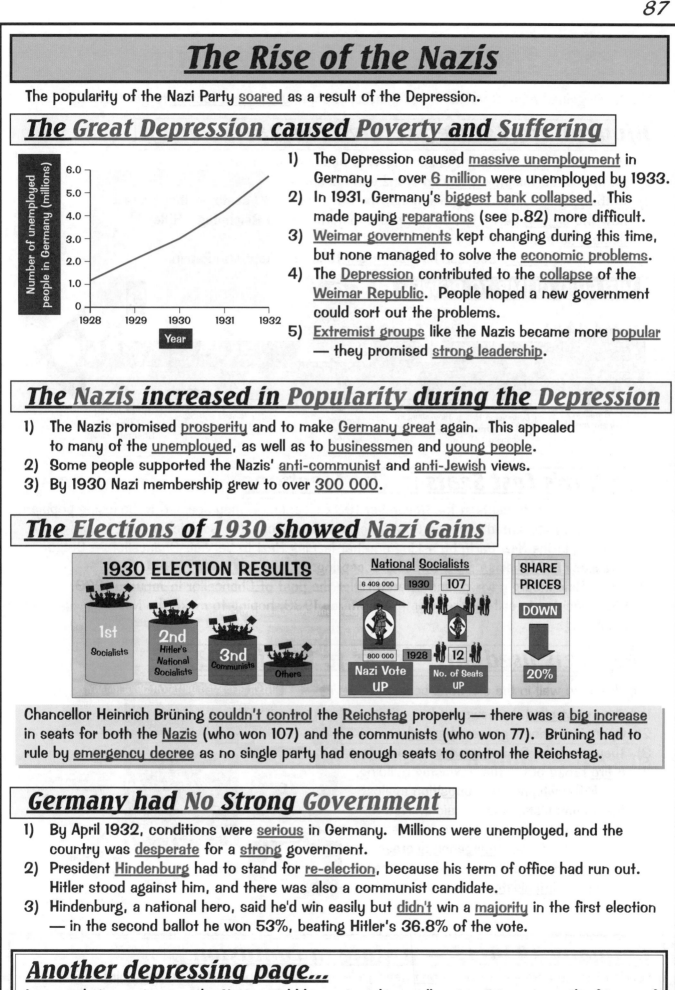

1) The Depression caused <u>massive unemployment</u> in Germany — over <u>6 million</u> were unemployed by 1933.
2) In 1931, Germany's <u>biggest bank collapsed</u>. This made paying <u>reparations</u> (see p.82) more difficult.
3) <u>Weimar governments</u> kept changing during this time, but none managed to solve the <u>economic problems</u>.
4) The <u>Depression</u> contributed to the <u>collapse</u> of the <u>Weimar Republic</u>. People hoped a new government could sort out the problems.
5) <u>Extremist groups</u> like the Nazis became more <u>popular</u> — they promised <u>strong leadership</u>.

The Nazis increased in Popularity during the Depression

1) The Nazis promised <u>prosperity</u> and to make <u>Germany great</u> again. This appealed to many of the <u>unemployed</u>, as well as to <u>businessmen</u> and <u>young people</u>.
2) Some people supported the Nazis' <u>anti-communist</u> and <u>anti-Jewish</u> views.
3) By 1930 Nazi membership grew to over <u>300 000</u>.

The Elections of 1930 showed Nazi Gains

Chancellor Heinrich Brüning <u>couldn't control</u> the <u>Reichstag</u> properly — there was a <u>big increase</u> in seats for both the <u>Nazis</u> (who won 107) and the communists (who won 77). Brüning had to rule by <u>emergency decree</u> as no single party had enough seats to control the Reichstag.

Germany had No Strong Government

1) By April 1932, conditions were <u>serious</u> in Germany. Millions were unemployed, and the country was <u>desperate</u> for a <u>strong</u> government.
2) President <u>Hindenburg</u> had to stand for <u>re-election</u>, because his term of office had run out. Hitler stood against him, and there was also a communist candidate.
3) Hindenburg, a national hero, said he'd win easily but <u>didn't</u> win a <u>majority</u> in the first election — in the second ballot he won 53%, beating Hitler's 36.8% of the vote.

Another depressing page...

In normal circumstances, the Nazis would have stayed a small, extremist group on the fringes of politics. Unfortunately the <u>Depression</u> gave them an <u>opportunity</u> to gain mainstream popularity.

The Rise of the Nazis

The Nazis gained a lot of votes — but they used some underhand tactics to get them...

Hindenburg Refused to give the Nazis Power

1) Hindenburg couldn't find a Chancellor who had support in the Reichstag.
2) He appointed the inexperienced Franz von Papen.
3) In the July 1932 Reichstag elections, the Nazis won 230 seats — they were now the biggest party, but didn't have a majority in the Reichstag. Hitler demanded to be made Chancellor.
4) Hindenburg refused because he didn't trust Hitler and kept von Papen.

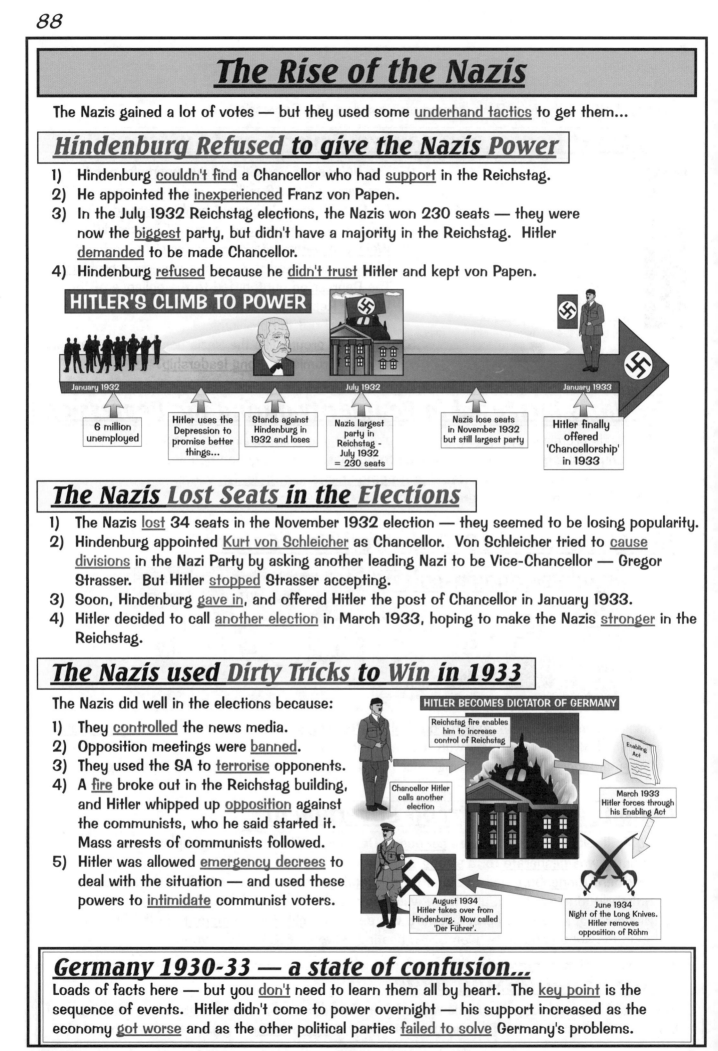

HITLER'S CLIMB TO POWER

January 1932 — 6 million unemployed — Hitler uses the Depression to promise better things... — Stands against Hindenburg in 1932 and loses — July 1932 — Nazis largest party in Reichstag - July 1932 = 230 seats — Nazis lose seats in November 1932 but still largest party — January 1933 — Hitler finally offered 'Chancellorship' in 1933

The Nazis Lost Seats in the Elections

1) The Nazis lost 34 seats in the November 1932 election — they seemed to be losing popularity.
2) Hindenburg appointed Kurt von Schleicher as Chancellor. Von Schleicher tried to cause divisions in the Nazi Party by asking another leading Nazi to be Vice-Chancellor — Gregor Strasser. But Hitler stopped Strasser accepting.
3) Soon, Hindenburg gave in, and offered Hitler the post of Chancellor in January 1933.
4) Hitler decided to call another election in March 1933, hoping to make the Nazis stronger in the Reichstag.

The Nazis used Dirty Tricks to Win in 1933

The Nazis did well in the elections because:

1) They controlled the news media.
2) Opposition meetings were banned.
3) They used the SA to terrorise opponents.
4) A fire broke out in the Reichstag building, and Hitler whipped up opposition against the communists, who he said started it. Mass arrests of communists followed.
5) Hitler was allowed emergency decrees to deal with the situation — and used these powers to intimidate communist voters.

HITLER BECOMES DICTATOR OF GERMANY

Chancellor Hitler calls another election — Reichstag fire enables him to increase control of Reichstag — Enabling Act — March 1933 Hitler forces through his Enabling Act — June 1934 Night of the Long Knives. Hitler removes opposition of Röhm — August 1934 Hitler takes over from Hindenburg. Now called 'Der Führer'.

Germany 1930-33 — a state of confusion...

Loads of facts here — but you don't need to learn them all by heart. The key point is the sequence of events. Hitler didn't come to power overnight — his support increased as the economy got worse and as the other political parties failed to solve Germany's problems.

Hitler Comes to Power

Once Hitler was Chancellor he set about strengthening his power...

Hitler Changed the Law to Keep Control

1) The Nazis won 288 seats but no majority — the communists still won 81.
2) So Hitler declared the Communist Party illegal.
3) This gave him enough support in parliament to bring in an Enabling Bill which was passed with threats and bargaining in March 1933.
4) This bill let him govern for four years without parliament and made all other parties illegal. Hitler was almost in full control.
5) Trade Unions were banned in May 1933.
6) In July 1933, all political parties, apart from the Nazi party, were banned in Germany.

The Night of the Long Knives

1) Hitler still had opposition — and was worried about rivals within the Nazi party.
2) The biggest threat was Ernst Röhm, who controlled the SA (over 400 000 men). On the 29th-30th June 1934, Hitler sent his own men to arrest Röhm and others. This became known as the 'Night of the Long Knives'.
3) Several hundred people were killed, including Röhm, Strasser and von Schleicher. Any potential opposition had been stamped out.
4) A month later Hindenburg died. Hitler combined the posts of Chancellor and President, made himself Commander-in-Chief of the army, and was called Der Führer (the leader). It was the beginning of dictatorship.

Germany was now under Strong Leaders

1) Germany was reorganised into a number of provinces. Each province was called a Gau (plural: Gaue), with a Gauleiter — a loyal Nazi — in charge of each.
2) Above them were the Reichsleiters who advised Hitler, e.g. Goebbels who was in charge of propaganda, and Himmler who was chief of the German police.
3) At the top was the Führer — Hitler himself — who was in absolute control.
4) Every aspect of life was carefully controlled, and only loyal Nazis could be successful.

Joseph Goebbels

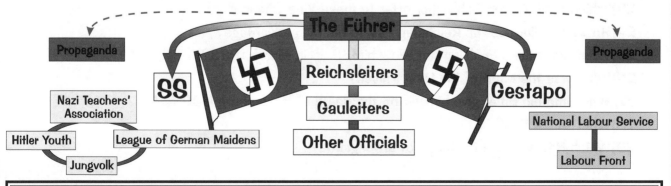

Hitler was obsessed with power...

Once elected the Nazis pretty quickly turned Germany from a democracy into a dictatorship. Hitler set himself up as a supreme ruler — Chancellor, President and army chief combined.

Revision Summary for Sections 1-2

Now's your chance to show off what you've learned — and to find out what you still need to practise. Make sure you know about the long-term consequences of the Versailles Treaty, and the reasons for the weakness of the Weimar government. You've also got to be able to give clear arguments for why Hitler was able to come to power. Remember — it doesn't matter if you can't answer all the questions first time. Go over the section again and keep trying, until you can answer every one first time. So let's get going.

1) What was the name of the clause which blamed Germany for starting World War One?

2) What is the name for the money Germany was meant to pay for the damage it caused?

3) What happened to Germany's overseas colonies after the war?

4) Which area of Germany did the Versailles Treaty ban the German military from?

5) What was the name of the first President of the Weimar Republic?

6) To which party did he belong?

7) Why was the government based at Weimar?

8) What is the name of the German Parliament?

9) Name the force which was set up to keep the peace in Germany.

10) Give three reasons for discontent in Germany after World War I.

11) Where did the Spartacist Revolt and the Kapp Putsch take place?

12) Give the main results of the French occupation of the Ruhr in 1923.

13) What was the name of the new currency introduced in Germany in 1924?

14) What was the name of the plan which reduced Germany's reparations bill by three-quarters?

15) Write a paragraph outlining the work of Gustav Stresemann.

16) In what year and in what country was Hitler born?

17) Who was the leader of the German Workers' Party when Hitler joined?

18) What was the name of the uprising Hitler led in 1923?

19) What was the title of the book Hitler wrote in prison?

20) Name the armed force which was set up to support the Nazis.

21) Where did the Nazis come in the 1930 election?

22) Who beat Hitler in the Presidential elections of April 1932?

23) Which Nazi did von Schleicher offer to make Vice-Chancellor?

24) How did Hitler use the Reichstag Fire to his own advantage?

25) What did Hitler's Enabling Act allow him to do in March 1933?

26) What was the Night of the Long Knives?

27) What title did Hitler give himself on the death of Hindenburg in 1934?

28) What was a Gau?

29) Which Nazi was put in charge of propaganda?

Nazi Propaganda

The Nazis wanted complete <u>control</u> over the German people —
they used propaganda to help them get it.

Propaganda aims to Control how people Think

1) Propaganda means spreading information that <u>influences</u> how people <u>think</u> and <u>behave</u>.
   It's a way of <u>shaping people's minds</u>.
2) It gives only certain <u>points of view</u> and often <u>leaves out important facts</u>.
3) The <u>Nazis</u> used <u>powerful propaganda</u> designed to get the support of the German people.

Goebbels took charge of Nazi Propaganda

1) The Nazis founded the <u>Ministry of Public Enlightenment and Propaganda</u> in <u>1933</u>.
   It was led by <u>Dr Joseph Goebbels</u>.
2) It had departments for <u>music</u>, <u>theatre</u>, <u>film</u>, <u>literature</u> and <u>radio</u>. All artists,
   writers, journalists and musicians had to <u>register</u> to get their <u>work approved</u>.
3) It tried to persuade everybody that the Nazis were <u>right</u>, and stop people reading
   or hearing anything that gave a <u>different message</u>.

The Nazis used Propaganda as a Method of Control

Nazi propaganda poster, 1935

1) The Nazis encouraged the German people to <u>hate</u> the
   countries that signed the <u>Treaty of Versailles</u>.
2) Nazi propaganda said that <u>Jews</u> and <u>communists</u> were the
   biggest cause of <u>Germany's problems</u>. One Nazi paper
   claimed that Jews <u>murdered children</u> for the Passover Feast.
3) Nazi propaganda was used to <u>unite</u> the German people, and
   make them believe the Nazis would make Germany <u>strong</u>.
4) Nazi propaganda took <u>simple ideas</u> and <u>repeated them</u>
   <u>constantly</u>.
5) Many German people were easier to persuade because the
   <u>Depression</u> had left them in <u>poverty</u>, and the Nazis promised
   to <u>help</u> them.

Nazis used the Media as a tool of Propaganda

1) The Nazis controlled the media, and decided what would be in the
   <u>newspapers</u>. They sold <u>cheap radios</u> to the people and <u>controlled</u>
   <u>the broadcasts</u>.
2) <u>Films</u> showed the strength of the Nazis and Hitler, and the weakness
   of opponents. An important German director was <u>Leni Riefenstahl</u>.
3) Another method of spreading propaganda was through <u>posters</u>
   showing the evil of Germany's enemies and the power of Hitler.

Don't believe everything you read...

The Nazis were very successful in getting the German people to follow them, even when things
weren't going well. A major part of their success was down to their skilled use of <u>propaganda</u>.
The image we have of the Nazis is very different from the one ordinary Germans had at the time.

Nazi Propaganda

Nazi propaganda was used to change <u>culture</u> and <u>society</u> in Germany.

Other Forms of propaganda were used

1) The Nazis used <u>public rallies</u> to spread their propaganda. The annual <u>Nuremberg Rallies</u> focused on speeches by leading Nazis, like Hitler and Goebbels. The 1934 Nuremberg Rally was recorded by Riefenstahl in her film <u>'Triumph of the Will'</u>.
2) One million people attended the 1936 rally. There were displays of <u>lights</u> and <u>flags</u> to greet the arrival of Hitler. These made him look <u>more powerful</u>.
3) Nazi power was also shown through <u>art</u> and <u>architecture</u> and grand new buildings appeared in Nuremberg and Berlin.
4) Sporting events like the <u>1936 Berlin Olympics</u> were used to show off German wealth and power. But Hitler was angered when the African-American athlete <u>Jesse Owens</u> won four gold medals.

Hitler was portrayed as the Saviour of Germany

1) Goebbels also created the <u>'Hitler Myth'</u> which made Hitler seem like a god and the saviour of Germany.
2) This was the <u>cult of the Führer</u>. Führer means <u>'Leader'</u> or <u>'Guide'</u>.
3) A popular slogan was <u>'One people, one empire, one leader'</u>.
4) The main purpose of the public rallies was to increase <u>loyalty to Hitler</u>.
5) Many Germans <u>devoted their lives</u> to Hitler.

Propaganda had a major effect on Society and Culture

1) Nazis tried to control <u>every aspect</u> of German life, including <u>religion</u>. Some priests who disagreed with the Nazis went to <u>concentration camps</u> (see p.100).
2) <u>School textbooks</u> made Germans look successful. Children were taught to believe in Nazi doctrines (see p.99).
3) The <u>'Strength through Joy'</u> programme sought to show ordinary workers that the Nazi regime cared about their conditions (see p.101).
4) The Nazis promised an empire that would last a <u>thousand years</u> — based on <u>traditional values</u>.
5) <u>Modern art</u> was banned, in favour of realistic paintings that fit with Nazi ideology. Modern art was labelled <u>degenerate</u> and exhibitions were created to show people how 'bad' it was.

6) The Nazis celebrated the works of <u>'German' composers</u>, such as Wagner, but much <u>modern classical music</u>, works by <u>Jewish composers</u>, and <u>jazz</u> were all attacked.

Society seemed Different to that of the Weimar Republic

1) The culture of the Weimar Republic had disappointed the more <u>old-fashioned</u> Germans. They thought <u>standards</u> in German society had slipped, and <u>welcomed</u> the Nazi approach.
2) People had <u>more freedom</u> under Weimar (see p.85) but Nazis thought this was harmful — they wanted to keep tight control over German society.
3) Workers and middle-class business people had suffered through <u>the Depression</u> under the Weimar Republic. Nazi promises of an <u>'economic miracle'</u> gave them hope.

We think about the Nazis quite differently...

The Nazis spent a lot of time putting together big, <u>stage-managed rallies</u> and parades. They managed to create a <u>powerful image</u> which still influences the way people think of them.

Censorship and Suppression

The Nazis wanted to get rid of all opposition within Germany.

The Nazis set up a Totalitarian State

1) In a <u>totalitarian state</u> the government has <u>complete control</u> over all aspects of life.
2) After weakening opposition in 1933, Hitler got the Reichstag to pass the <u>Enabling Act</u> that gave him <u>unlimited power</u> to pass laws.
3) In <u>July 1933</u>, all political parties except the Nazi Party were <u>banned</u>. The <u>Law for Reconstruction of the Reich</u> (1934) gave the Nazis total power over <u>the state governments</u> — the local governments in Germany's regions, such as in Bavaria, Saxony and Hesse.

Germany became a Police State

1) The <u>SS</u> (<u>Schutzstaffel</u>) began as a bodyguard for Hitler. It expanded massively under the leadership of Himmler during the 1930s. Its members were totally loyal to Hitler, and feared for their <u>cruelty</u>. Himmler was also in charge of the <u>secret police</u> — the <u>Gestapo</u>.
2) After 1933 <u>concentration camps</u> spread across Germany and its territories to hold political prisoners and anybody else considered dangerous to the Nazis. Some of these were later turned into <u>death camps</u> (see p.96).
3) Local <u>wardens</u> were employed to make sure Germans were loyal to the Nazis. People were encouraged to <u>report disloyalty</u>. Many were arrested by the Gestapo as a result.

Censorship helped to Stifle Opposition

1) Over <u>25 000 books</u> were burned in a <u>single night</u> in 1933 including the work of Jewish writers like Einstein. This attracted <u>protests</u> in other countries.
2) All <u>newspapers</u> and other media were put under the control of the <u>Ministry of Public Enlightenment and Propaganda</u>. Only news <u>favourable</u> to the Nazis was allowed.
3) Jews were forbidden from <u>owning</u> or <u>publishing newspapers</u> and anybody could be <u>executed</u> for publishing anti-Nazi works.

Hitler attacked all groups that might Oppose the Nazis

1) In 1934, during the <u>Night of the Long Knives</u>, Hitler had many leaders killed whom he considered dangerous, including <u>Ernst Röhm</u>, leader of the SA, and <u>General von Schleicher</u>.
2) Hitler also tried to bring the Churches under control (see p.100). Members of some religious groups like the <u>Jehovah's Witnesses</u> were sent to concentration camps.
3) <u>Trade unions</u> were <u>abolished</u> in 1933 and the <u>German Labour Front</u> was set up to include workers and employers. <u>Strikes</u> became <u>illegal</u>.

The Nazis used <u>concentration camps</u> to remove anyone they did not like including disabled people, homosexuals, Jews and communists. Some of these became <u>extermination camps</u>.

This book wouldn't be available in Nazi Germany...

Take a copy of a national newspaper and count how many stories the Nazis wouldn't have allowed. Anything <u>criticising</u> the government would be out. There'd be <u>very little</u> paper left.

Nazi Belief in a Master Race

The Nazi belief in the idea of a Master Race caused great harm to many minorities.

Nazis believed Aryans were the Germans' Ancestors

1) Most Nazis believed that Northern Europeans, including Germans, were members of an ancient race called the Aryans. These ideas came from nineteenth-century writers who argued that the Aryans were a superior race. Some thought Aryans could be identified by measuring the shape of their heads and faces.

2) Nazis thought people under German rule who were not pure Aryans did not belong. They were weakening 'pure' German people.

3) Hitler wanted to 'cleanse' the German people by removing anybody who spoiled the 'purity' of the Aryan race. These included Jews and Romani (gypsies).

4) In 1931 the SS started a Race and Settlement Office to decide which individuals were 'pure' enough for them to marry. In 1935 the Nuremberg Laws were based on the idea that Jews were biologically different from Germans (see next page).

A Master Race would need more Space

1) Hitler believed that the German people needed more land — Lebensraum (living space). This was the main reason for the invasion of Eastern Europe. Hitler believed much of this new space would be taken from the USSR.

2) The idea of Volksgemeinschaft was that all people would serve the Reich together as a community rather than just living there. This would lead to a union of pure-Germanic people working together for a Greater Germany.

3) People who weren't considered Aryans could play no part in the new German empire. Some Jews were given passports to leave Germany but not to return.

Nazi ideas of a Master Race harmed many people

1) Jews were not the only group accused of spoiling the purity of the German people. Hitler saw Romani (gypsies) as a racial threat. There were about 30 000 in Germany. Many were sent to concentration camps.

2) People with mental and physical disabilities were targeted by the Nazis — many were murdered or sterilised.

3) Under the Nazis over 400 000 people were forcibly sterilised to stop them having children. People of mixed race were also attacked by the Nazis — many were sterilised against their will.

4) Homosexual people were sent to concentration camps in their thousands. In 1936, Himmler, Head of the SS, began the Central Office for the Combating of Homosexuality and Abortion.

When terrible theories get put into practice...

The Nazis had a whole range of crazy theories to justify their international aggression and the persecution of ordinary Germans. It's worth learning these points as they help explain why the Nazis ended up forcing Germany into a huge and costly war.

Persecution of the Jews

The Nazis took away more and more of the civil rights of the Jews.

The Nazis Hated the Jews

Hitler always claimed the Jews were responsible for many German problems, and harsh laws were passed against them from the time he became Chancellor in 1933.

| 1933 — The Nazis murdered 36 Jews. Over 35 000 Jews fled Germany. | 1935 — Nuremberg Laws — Jews could not vote or marry Germans. | Concentration Camps established. | 1938 November — "Night of Broken Glass". Jewish shops, homes and synagogues attacked. | 1939 — Increased control. A curfew was introduced. Jews could no longer own radios. | 1941 — Jews were made to wear a yellow star. They were banned from public transport and had their rations reduced. |

In 1935 the Nazis Passed the Nuremberg Laws

1) These laws stopped Jews being German citizens.
2) They banned marriage between Jews and non-Jews in Germany.
3) They also banned sexual relationships between Jews and non-Jews.

Many Jews went into exile, such as Albert Einstein — they spoke out against the Nazi regime from abroad, but the world did nothing.

Kristallnacht 1938 — The Night of the Broken Glass

1) A Jew murdered a German diplomat in Paris in November 1938.
2) There was rioting throughout Germany — thousands of Jewish shops were smashed, and thousands of Jews were arrested.
3) Nazi propaganda made people believe that the Jews were bad for Germany, so they should be sent to special Concentration Camps, or humiliated and maltreated in public.
4) Many people believed the camps were work-camps, where the Jews would work for Germany. Later, Nazi policy became more terrible as they tried to exterminate the Jewish race.

The Nazis encouraged people to boycott Jewish-owned shops. The graffiti says 'Jude' — the German word for 'Jew'.

There was little German Opposition to the persecution

It's hard to understand why so few people protested — there were four main reasons:

1) Everybody was scared of the SS and the Gestapo.
2) People were better off after years of hardship, and chose to ignore what they didn't like.
3) Goebbels' propaganda was so effective that people didn't get the whole story about what was really going on — but believed the Nazi government knew best.
4) Opponents, like the communists, had been eliminated.

Nazi Germany — a climate of cruelty and fear...

The Jewish people suffered terribly at the hands of the Nazis — and you need to know how. This is horrific, and it's hard to understand why most Germans didn't protest. Remember — it wasn't just the Jews who were persecuted, but also the Romani, homosexuals, Slavic peoples and others.

The Holocaust

The Nazi regime became more murderous as the war went on.

The War made Nazi Persecution worse

1) After the invasions of Poland and Russia more Jews came under Nazi control.
2) Adolf Eichmann was put in charge of dealing with these Jews.
3) In 1940 the idea of deporting all the Jews from Europe to a Jewish reservation was dropped. Instead they were moved into ghettos — small areas in cities where Jews were forced to live in overcrowded, unsanitary conditions. The largest ghetto was in Warsaw. Starvation and disease killed hundreds of thousands.
4) When Russia was invaded in 1941, Special Action Corps followed the army with orders to kill every Jew they came across in the occupied towns and villages.

The Nazis began the Final Solution in 1942

1) The Final Solution was the Nazis' plan to destroy the Jewish people.
2) Death camps were built in Eastern Europe. Gas chambers were built for mass murder.
3) Mainly Jewish people were killed, but other groups were targeted as well, for example Slavs (Russians and Poles), Romani, black people, homosexuals, disabled people and communists.
4) Heinrich Himmler, head of the SS, was in overall charge of this 'final solution'.
5) Some extermination camps were: Auschwitz, Treblinka, Sobibor, Chelmno, Belzec.
6) By the end of the war, approximately 6 million Jewish people had been killed by the Nazis.

It's hard to understand How this Mass Murder happened

After the war, people around the world found it hard to believe that this inhuman, cold-blooded extermination had taken place, and that so many soldiers were involved. It has been argued:
1) The Nazi guards were doing a job and obeying orders. They feared their leaders.
2) The Jews were not regarded as human by the Nazis — killing them didn't matter to guards.
3) The soldiers involved hid the truth of what they were doing. The world only discovered the horror of the Death Camps as the Allies advanced in 1945.

The Reaction of the Jewish People

1) They faced death for any resistance. Some fled into the forests, and formed resistance groups to blow up railway lines and attack German soldiers.
2) In some ghettos Jewish authorities thought the best way to save lives was to cooperate with the Nazis and to produce goods for them.
3) A rebellion in the Warsaw ghetto in 1943 was ruthlessly put down.
4) There was some resistance in the camps, and escapes from Sobibor and Auschwitz.
5) Reports of what was happening in the camps were smuggled out. Before the war ended, Nazi orders went out to destroy the camps and the evidence — but there wasn't time.

Some historians claim there's evidence leaders like Churchill were told about the camps — and didn't believe the facts. By April 1945 approximately 6 million Jewish people had been murdered.

Holocaust means "Sacrifice" — Shoah means "Catastrophe"...

Holocaust is a term disliked by some Jewish people, who prefer to use the word Shoah. The Nazis organised and carried out murder on an industrial scale — deliberately killing millions and millions of people.

Opposition to the Nazis

The Nazis had a tight grip on Germany, but some opposition remained.

Opposition was Weak under the Nazis

1) Most people who disagreed with the Nazis were afraid of the SS and the Gestapo. They were also afraid their friends and neighbours would inform on them if they criticised the regime.
2) Thousands of those who did voice opposition to the Nazis were sent to concentration camps.
3) Opposition within the Party was crushed on the Night of the Long Knives (p.89).
4) Anti-Nazi activity had to be carried out in secret — which made it difficult for different groups to work together.
5) Nazi propaganda persuaded most people that they were better off under Hitler.

The Nazis Overcame most Resistance

1) Once in power, the Nazis banned communist groups and sent many communists to concentration camps.
2) Some opposition came from religious groups, especially after church land was confiscated.
3) Jehovah's Witnesses were persecuted for not supporting the regime, with many members sent to the concentration camps.
4) Some opponents of the Reich Church joined together as the Confessing Church. Over 6000 clergy were arrested, including Martin Niemöller, one of the Confessing Church's founders.
5) Catholic dissent was more widespread after 1937, when Pope Pius XI sent out a letter protesting at German nationalism and racism, which was read out in Catholic churches.
6) Catholic protesters had some success in reducing Nazi interference with the Church.

Not all Young People supported the Nazis

1) The Edelweiss Pirates were groups of rebellious young people who were difficult to control. They didn't like being told what to do, and used the slogan 'Everlasting war on Hitler Youth'.
2) Some Edelweiss Pirates even sided with the Allies during the war and several were executed.
3) Other groups, like the Swing Kids who liked banned jazz music, were more a nuisance than a serious threat.
4) In Munich in 1943, a group of students called the White Rose were arrested after distributing anti-Nazi leaflets. Several, including Sophie and Hans Scholl, were executed.

Resistance in the Army grew during the War

1) As the war started to go badly, some believed Hitler was leading Germany to defeat.
2) There had been plots against Hitler from the army officers before the war, but these became more serious after the German defeats at El Alamein and Stalingrad in 1942.
3) One of the most famous army plots led to Claus von Stauffenberg's attempt to kill Hitler. He put a bomb in a meeting room, but Hitler survived and most of the plotters were executed in 1944.

It wasn't easy to stand against the Nazis...

In the end, it was losing the war which toppled the Nazis — not German resistance.

Revision Summary for Sections 3-4

A pretty grim couple of sections, I'm afraid — but that doesn't mean you don't have to learn them thoroughly like the others. Here are loads of practice questions to make sure you've learnt it all. Use the same method as always... answer the questions, check your answers against the sections, then try them again and again until you can get them all right without checking.

1) Write a short definition of propaganda.

2) Who was put in charge of the Ministry of Public Enlightenment and Propaganda?

3) Which groups did Nazi propaganda attack?

4) Name an important film director in Nazi Germany.

5) In which German city were the biggest Nazi rallies held?

6) In which year did the Berlin Olympics take place?

7) Which African-American athlete won four gold medals at the Berlin Olympics?

8) How long did the Nazis imagine their empire would last?

9) Briefly describe the Nazi policy on art.

10) Who was the leader of the SS?

11) What was the name of the Nazi secret police?

12) In what year were trade unions abolished in Germany?

13) Which organisation was set up to replace the trade unions in Nazi Germany?

14) What was the name of the ethnic group the Nazis claimed to be a part of?

15) Briefly explain what Lebensraum means.

16) Which 1935 laws officially declared Jews to be non-Germans?

17) What other restrictions did these laws bring in?

18) Name an ethnic group other than the Jews who the Nazis persecuted.

19) What event was used as an excuse for the anti-Semitic rioting of the Night of Broken Glass?

20) Give two possible reasons why most Germans didn't protest against the persecution of the Jews.

21) What were the ghettos?

22) Who was placed in overall charge of the 'final solution'?

23) In which ghetto was there a rebellion against the Nazis in 1943?

24) What is the meaning of the Hebrew word 'Shoah' in English?

25) Give three reasons why German opposition to the Nazis was weak.

26) Name the Church that was set up in opposition to the official Reich Church.

27) In what year did Pope Pius XI send out a letter protesting against Nazi policies?

28) Members of which group were arrested in Munich in 1943 after handing out anti-Nazi leaflets?

29) Which two major military defeats encouraged the German army to plot more seriously against Hitler?

30) Who placed the bomb which was meant to kill Hitler in a meeting room in 1944?

Young People

An important key to Nazi success was to control the minds of German youth.

Youth Movements helped produce Committed Nazis

1) Hitler knew that loyalty from young people was essential if the Nazis were to remain strong.
2) Youth movements were a way of teaching children Nazi ideas — so they would be loyal to the Nazi Party when they grew up.
3) Propaganda claimed that young people were more likely to be successful under the Nazis than they had been in the Weimar Republic.

1) The Hitler Youth was founded in 1926. Boys aged fourteen and over were recruited to the movement. It became compulsory in 1936.
2) The Hitler Youth became part of the SA (see p.86). Promising boys might be sent to Hitler Schools where they were trained to lead.
3) Boys wore military-style uniforms and took part in physical exercise preparing for war. Many later joined the army.
4) Girls between fourteen and eighteen joined the League of German Maidens. Girls were trained in domestic skills like sewing and cooking. Sometimes they took part in physical activities like camping and hiking.

5) A Reich Youth Leader was introduced in 1933 and youth movements increased in importance.
6) During the Second World War, members of the Hitler Youth contributed to the war effort — for example, helping with air defence work, farm work and collecting donations for Nazi charities.

Nazis took over in Schools and Universities

1) Education in schools meant learning Nazi propaganda. No Jewish people could teach in schools or universities. Most teachers joined the Nazi Teachers' Association and were trained in Nazi methods. Children had to report teachers who did not use them.
2) Subjects like history and biology were rewritten to fit in with Nazi ideas. Children were taught to be anti-Semitic and that the First World War was lost because of Jews and communists.
3) Physical education became more important for boys, sometimes playing war games with live ammunition.
4) In universities students burned anti-Nazi and Jewish books, and Jewish lecturers were sacked. Education across Germany was 'Nazified'.

The Hitler Youth — not quite the Boys' Brigade...

...or the Scouts, or the Woodcraft Folk. But its appeal wasn't so different — camping, bonfires, all that kind of stuff. It's worth remembering that although the Nazis put a sinister spin on their youth groups, they were filled with ordinary people who weren't necessarily zealous Nazis. After 1939 all young people ended up in Nazi youth movements — even those who weren't so keen.

Women and the Church

The Nazis wanted women to be homemakers.

Women were expected to raise Large Families

1) Nazis didn't want women to have too much freedom. They believed the role of women was to support their families at home. Women existed to provide children.
2) The League of German Maidens spread the Nazi idea that it was an honour to produce large families for Germany. Nazis gave awards to women for doing this.
3) At school, girls studied subjects like cookery. It was stressed that they should choose 'Aryan' husbands.
4) Women were banned from being lawyers in 1936 and the Nazis did their best to stop them following other professions. But the shortage of workers after 1937 meant more women had to go back to work.

The Nazis saw the Church as a Threat

1) Many Nazis were against Christianity — its teaching of peace was seen as incompatible with Nazi ideas. However, the Nazis didn't want to risk an immediate attack on it.
2) Hitler signed an agreement with the Catholic Church in 1933. Each side promised not to interfere with the other. However the Nazis did try to curb the influence of the Church — and there were some Catholic protests against Nazi policies.
3) Hitler tried to unite the different Protestant Churches into one Reich Church. He placed the Nazi Bishop Ludwig Müller at its head. Some Church members split off in protest at this state interference. They formed the Confessing Church.
4) Many clergy who stood up to the Nazi regime were sent to concentration camps.

Most Church members Supported the Nazis

There was little opposition in Germany to the Nazis from Christian groups. Many Christians supported Hitler because he stopped the spread of communism — which was actively hostile to religion. There were, however, a number of Church members who did oppose the Nazis:

1) Martin Niemöller was a Lutheran minister, a decorated World War One U-boat captain, and a one-time Nazi supporter. He objected to Nazi interference in the Church, and was one of the founders of the Confessing Church, which stood against the Nazi-backed Reich Church. He used a sermon in 1937 to protest against the persecution of Church members — and as a result spent the rest of the Nazi years in concentration camps.
2) Clemens August von Galen was the Catholic Bishop of Münster, who used his sermons to protest about the 'euthanasia' of the disabled and against Nazi racial policies. Only the need to maintain the support of German Catholics stopped the Nazis from executing him.
3) Another key member of the Confessing Church was Dietrich Bonhoeffer, a Lutheran theologian and pastor who opposed the Nazis from the beginning. He joined the resistance — helping Jews escape from Germany, and plotting to kill Hitler. He was caught and spent over a year in prison before he was executed just weeks before the fall of the Nazis.

I Confess — I'm pretty sick of the Nazis...

The Churches are important when looking at opposition to the Nazis as they were among the few organisations that — to a limited extent at least — could stand up to the Nazis. Because most Germans were Christians at the time, the Nazis couldn't just stamp them out completely. This was even more true after the union with Austria, which was overwhelmingly Catholic.

Economic Growth under the Nazis

The Nazis took strict <u>control</u> of the economy.

Hitler gave *Work to Millions of Unemployed*

1) Hitler started a huge <u>programme</u> of <u>public works</u>, which gave <u>jobs</u> to thousands of people.
2) From 1933, huge motorways — <u>Autobahns</u> — were started. <u>Unemployment fell</u> dramatically.
3) But — the Nazis also <u>fiddled with the statistics</u> to make unemployment look <u>lower</u> than it really was. E.g. they didn't count women or Jewish people in the unemployment statistics — this is called "<u>invisible unemployment</u>".

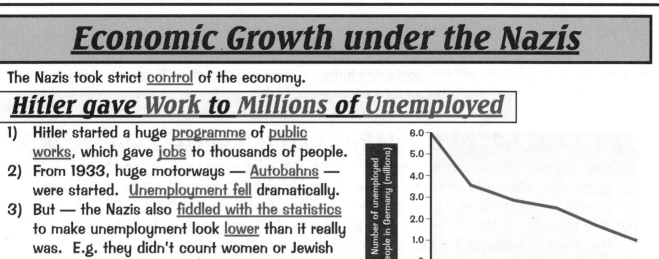

People were *Encouraged to Work by Rewards*

1) <u>All</u> men between 18 and 25 could be <u>recruited</u> into the <u>National Labour Service</u> and given jobs.
2) The Nazis got rid of trade unions. Instead workers had to join the Nazis' <u>Labour Front</u>.
3) The Nazis introduced '<u>Strength through Joy</u>' — a scheme which provided workers with <u>cheap holidays</u> and leisure activities. Another scheme, '<u>Beauty of Labour</u>', encouraged factory owners to <u>improve conditions</u> for their workers.
4) Output increased in Germany, and <u>unemployment</u> was almost <u>ended</u> completely. The Nazis introduced the <u>Volkswagen</u> (the people's car) as an <u>ambition</u> for people to aim for.
5) <u>Wages</u> were still relatively <u>low</u> though — and workers <u>weren't allowed</u> to go on <u>strike</u> or campaign for better conditions.

The *New Plan* made Germany more *Self Sufficient*

1) Germany's industrial growth meant it was buying more raw materials from abroad. Germany was <u>importing</u> a lot more than it was <u>exporting</u>, which caused <u>economic problems</u>.
2) The Minister of the Economy, <u>Schacht</u>, brought in the <u>New Plan</u> in 1934.
3) This <u>strictly controlled</u> imports and encouraged exports — the aim was to make Germany more <u>self sufficient</u>. Production increased and unemployment fell.
4) Schacht eventually <u>resigned</u> because he felt the increased focus on <u>weapons production</u> was damaging the economy. Control of the economy fell to <u>Göring</u>.

Hitler Re-armed the *Germany Military*

1) The Nazis built up the army <u>secretly</u> at first, because it was breaking the <u>Treaty of Versailles</u>.
2) Hitler <u>sacked</u> some of the generals, and <u>replaced</u> them with Nazi supporters. Göring was put in charge of the <u>Luftwaffe</u> (air force), which had been banned at Versailles.
3) In 1935, <u>military conscription</u> was reintroduced (drafting men into the army).
4) In 1936, the Nazis introduced a <u>Four-Year Plan</u> to <u>prepare</u> the country for <u>war</u>. <u>Industrial production</u> increased — many workers had to <u>retrain</u> in jobs that would help the war effort.
5) The plan was to make Germany a <u>self-sufficient</u> country (an "autarky") so it wasn't reliant on foreign goods. They especially wanted to be self sufficient in the <u>raw materials</u> needed for <u>war</u>. But by 1939, Germany was still importing about a third of its raw materials.

Hitler reduced unemployment — and gained popularity...

Hitler provided new jobs and helped Germany recover from the <u>Depression</u> (see p.87).

A Social Revolution

Nazi policies can be viewed as a social revolution — radically changing German society.
But it's debatable how much things really changed.

The Nazis hoped to change German Society completely

1) Nazi policies affected many aspects of society like education, working conditions and law and order. Nazi ideas also had a big impact on people's attitudes and the way certain social groups were treated — e.g. their ideas about the 'master race' or the role of women.

2) Nazi propaganda spread the idea that society was changing completely. They portrayed themselves as defying the Treaty of Versailles to bring pride back to the people.

3) The economic recovery in the mid-1930s made it seem like people's lives were improving.

4) The Nazi ideal of Volksgemeinschaft — a perfect community of the people working hard towards the same aims — seemed attractive to lots of people.

5) To some extent the Nazis broke down old divisions between social classes.

The Nazis Didn't Change every aspect of German Society

1) Nazis did make a difference to society, but the changes were not always deep. Nazi propaganda made changes seem greater than they were.

2) It wasn't always necessary to join the Nazi Party. Many people in important positions kept their jobs without being members, for example Schacht the Minister of the Economy.

3) Some parents didn't want their children to join Nazi youth movements. Many Germans resisted Nazi propaganda. But it was dangerous to be openly against the Nazis.

4) Some of the changes introduced by the Nazis such as health reforms were started during the Weimar Republic, but the Nazis claimed them as theirs.

5) The Nazis discriminated against many social groups, e.g. Jews, communists, Romani and people with disabilities. The Nazis' vision for Germany excluded many groups.

6) There were still strong social divisions between classes, despite the ideal of Volksgemeinschaft.

Many groups in society Felt Better Off

1) Nazis focused on gaining the support of the workers in Germany. Campaigns like Strength through Joy and the Beauty of Labour made workers feel important. One third of all workers had been unemployed in the Great Depression under the Weimar Republic.

2) The value of Germany's production went up from 58 000 million marks in 1932 to 93 000 million marks in 1937. Workers were made to feel an essential part of the Volksgemeinschaft.

3) Small-business owners were able to advance more in society than under Weimar where class differences were stronger. This appealed to the middle classes.

> But workers and small-business owners were not really better off. The cost of living rose by about 25% — but wages didn't go up. Trade Unions were banned, as was the right to strike or resign. Small businesses had to pay high taxes.

Volksgemeinschaft — not the people's pits...

So, people in Germany were encouraged to feel better even though, in many cases, things for them were getting worse — that's the joy to be had with propaganda. Of course, then the war came and then everything got a bit more scary. Not that it wasn't scary enough already...

Impact of the Second World War

The Nazis prepared for war — but they weren't yet at full strength when the Second World War broke out in 1939.

The Nazi Economy had to Prepare for War

1) In 1936 Göring was put in charge of the economy. He aimed to make Germany self sufficient — so it could produce enough goods and raw materials to not need imports.
2) Hitler combined economic and military policy. The economy was being geared to war.
3) A Four-Year Plan started in 1936 concentrated on war preparations.
4) Many workers were retrained to do jobs that would help the war effort, such as producing weapons and working in chemical plants.

The Outbreak of War forced Changes in the Economy

1) At the start of the Second World War, the German economy wasn't ready.
2) Production geared to war was increased at the expense of domestic goods. The Nazis needed to build up industries like weapons and chemicals, and increase Germany's agricultural output, quickly.
3) By the outbreak of war a quarter of the workforce was busy on work for the war effort, especially on weapons. Two years later this had become three-quarters. Working hours increased to over 50 hours per week.

4) Production was often inefficient. Germany took raw materials from occupied lands in the East and used slave labour to keep its war effort going. In 1942 Hitler put Albert Speer in charge of the war economy.
5) By focusing the economy more completely on the war effort and by increasing efficiency, Speer greatly increased weapons production. But Allied bombing was taking an increasing toll on German industry.

The Outbreak of War had a dramatic Effect on Society

1) At first, most Germans didn't suffer badly because of the war — but they did make sacrifices to help the war effort by working longer hours for wages that were lower than they'd been under the Weimar Republic.
2) Millions of foreign workers were brought into Germany. Some business people resented the outbreak of war, especially with rationing of clothes and food introduced in 1939.
3) More women and children had to work, especially after 1941 when German forces were doing badly in Russia. Civilians were soon being killed through Allied bombing raids.

The end of the war meant the end for the Nazis...

It's impossible to know how long the Nazis would have lasted for if they hadn't got involved in a war, or if they'd won. Although they may not have changed Germany as much as they wanted, it was a very different place in the 1940s than in the 1920s. Hitler's control over the country only ended when he killed himself as the Russians approached Berlin in 1945.

Revision Summary for Section 5

That's the Nazis finished then — hooray. Life was very different for ordinary Germans under the Nazi regime compared to the Weimar Republic. The Nazis succeeded in making the German economy and army strong again. There were big changes, but at a terrible cost. Your job is to learn it all. And to help with it here are some questions. It's the usual drill. Answer the questions, check your answers against the section, then keep repeating until you can get them all correct...

1) In what year did membership of the Hitler Youth become compulsory for German boys?

2) What was the Nazi youth organisation for girls called?

3) What organisation did teachers have to join?

4) What happened to books by Jewish authors at the universities during the Nazi period?

5) What did the Nazis think the role of women should be?

6) In which year were women banned from being lawyers?

7) Who did Hitler appoint as head of the Reich Church?

8) Write a brief summary of the work of one Church minister who stood up to the Nazis.

9) Who were the "invisible unemployed" under the Nazis?

10) What did the Strength through Joy programme provide for German workers?

11) Why did the Nazis begin their rearmament secretly?

12) What does 'autarky' mean?

13) What was meant by Volksgemeinschaft?

14) Why does Nazi propaganda give a false impression about the depth of changes German society went through?

15) Give two reasons why some Germans may have felt positive about Nazi changes to the economy.

16) Why did some Germans have to retrain in the late 1930s?

17) What fraction of the workforce was employed in the war effort at the start of the war?

18) Who did Hitler put in charge of the war economy in 1942?

How to Study History

You've learnt the <u>facts</u> — now you need to learn how to <u>use them</u> effectively. There are <u>four key ideas</u> that'll help you use your facts — the four 'C's: Cause, Consequence, Change, Continuity.

You'll get Questions about <u>Causes</u> and <u>Consequences</u>

1) <u>Cause</u> means the <u>reason</u> something happened — e.g. why the Nazi Party rose to power. Any time you have an event in History, think about <u>what</u> caused it and <u>why</u> it happened. There are always reasons why an event takes place and it's your job to work them out.

2) <u>Consequence</u> means what happened <u>because</u> of an action — it's the <u>result</u> of an event, e.g. one consequence of the California Gold Rush was damage to the environment.

> 1) Some questions will ask you to give an <u>opinion</u>, e.g. "Who contributed most to the progress of medical knowledge: the Ancient Egyptians or the Ancient Greeks? Give reasons for your answer." or "How important was Hitler's leadership in the Nazis' rise to power?"
>
> 2) It's up to you what <u>opinion</u> you give — but you've got to be able to <u>back it up</u> with <u>reasons</u> and <u>facts</u>.

You also need to think about <u>Change</u> and <u>Continuity</u>

1) <u>Change</u> is when something happens to make things <u>different</u> — there can be <u>quick</u> changes, e.g. the Night of the Long Knives wiped out all internal opposition in the Nazi Party. Or there can be <u>slow</u> changes, e.g. the gradual settlement of the Great Plains by white settlers.

2) <u>Continuity</u> is the <u>opposite</u> of change — it means when things stay the <u>same</u>, e.g. during the "Dark Ages" in Britain (c.410-1066 AD) medical knowledge didn't progress much at all.

3) These ideas are opposites — think of <u>continuity</u> as a <u>flat line</u> going along until there is a sudden <u>change</u> and the line becomes a <u>zigzag</u>:

> Use the four 'C's in your answers — <u>link facts</u> together and tell the examiners <u>why</u> something happened and what the <u>results</u> were. <u>Explain</u> if there was a change and if so, what things changed from and what they changed to.

Time for some exam tips...

Obviously, you're going to need to <u>learn</u> all the info for your topics. But to get <u>high marks</u>, you need to do more than just trot out the facts. You need to be able to discuss topics in a thoughtful way, showing good understanding. The four 'C's are really useful for this.

Handling Sources

There are few certainties in life — but you will get source questions in your exam...

There are Two Main Kinds of Sources

1) Primary sources — this is evidence from the period you're studying, e.g. a Nazi propaganda poster.
2) Secondary sources — this is evidence about a historical period, e.g. a 1989 book entitled 'Hitler's Germany'.
3) Sources may be visual extracts, e.g. photographs and maps, or written extracts, e.g. diaries, newspapers etc.

If You Want to Do Well Look at Sources Carefully

1) You've got to find evidence from the source which is relevant to the question.
2) Show you understand the source, and use the facts you already know about the period to explain what the source is saying, and how it says it.
3) Say how reliable and useful you think the source is. Think about whether the source gives enough information about the topic or if there are gaps or inconsistencies. Say if you think the source is biased (one-sided in its opinions) — and if so, why.

> Don't confuse facts and opinions — always think about who is writing, why they are writing and what they are trying to say. Think about what their attitudes are to what they're writing about.

Top Tips for Answering Source Questions

Do
1) Use the source material to help answer the question — don't just rely on what you know already.
2) Read the question carefully. E.g. if it says to use three sources A, B and C, you must use all three.
3) If you're asked to look at more than one source, then compare them.
4) Check what the source tells you — look out for what a source says, who wrote it and when they wrote it.
5) Use the facts you already know about the period to help you understand the source and judge how useful it is.

Don't
1) Don't get carried away writing down everything you know about the topic — focus on the source(s) given.
2) Don't jump to conclusions — e.g. don't assume that every eyewitness account is accurate.
3) Don't always take sources at face value. E.g. school books from Nazi Germany might blame Jews and communists for the First World War. You've got to think about the attitudes of the people who created the source.

Historians love ketchup — they're obsessed with sources...

Evaluating sources is an important skill for historians — and one you have to demonstrate in the exam. So if you want decent grades, put the effort into learning this page right now.

Exam Essay Skills

You've also got to be able to tackle <u>essay answers</u>...

Planning Your Exam Time

1) On the exam paper, it'll say next to each question <u>how many marks</u> it's worth.
2) Look out for which questions have <u>most marks</u> — make sure you spend <u>most time</u> on these.
3) There'll be at least one or two questions which require <u>essay-length</u> answers.

> <u>Learn the rule</u> — the <u>more marks</u> a question is worth, the <u>longer</u> your answer should be. Don't get carried away writing loads for a question that's only worth 4 marks — you need to <u>leave time</u> for the higher mark questions.

Remember these *Three Tips* for writing good Essays

1) Plan your Essay

<u>Sort out</u> what you want to say before you start writing — think about <u>how to answer the question</u>, and what the <u>key words</u> are. Scribble a <u>quick plan</u> of your main points — <u>cross through this neatly</u> at the end, so it's obvious it shouldn't be marked.

Q3b) Plan
- intro - open range   - cattle rustling / branding
  v. homesteads   Johnson County war
- barbed wire   - concl. - several reasons but
- Texas fever   barbed wire / fencing off most
- bad winter 1886-7   important
There were several factors which contributed to the conflict
between homesteaders and cattlemen but the most important

2) Stay Focused on the Question

Make sure that you <u>directly answer the question</u>. <u>Back up your points</u> with relevant facts. Don't just chuck in everything you know. You've got to be <u>relevant</u> and <u>accurate</u> — e.g. if you're writing about the impact of World War II on Germany, don't include stories about a London camel called George who moved rubble during the Blitz.

3) Use a Clear Writing Style

Your essay should start with a brief <u>introduction</u> and end with a <u>conclusion</u>. Remember to start a <u>new paragraph</u> for each new point you want to discuss. Try to use <u>clear handwriting</u> — and pay attention to <u>spelling</u>, <u>grammar</u> and <u>punctuation</u>.

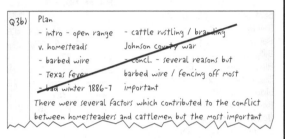

1) introduction
2) content
3) conclusion

Read through your answer and Correct any Mistakes

1) If you've made a <u>mistake</u> — <u>don't panic</u>. <u>Cross out</u> the mistake <u>neatly</u>. Write the <u>correction</u> above the mistake.

> Goebbels
> (~~Goering~~) was in charge of propaganda.

2) If you've <u>missed something out</u>, you can put an <u>asterisk</u> (*) beside where it should go, and then another asterisk with the missing information either in the <u>margin</u> or at the <u>end of your essay</u>.

> *in 1864 | 163 people were killed in the massacre.*

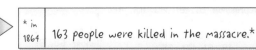

There's no need to panic in the exam...

Stay calm, <u>read the questions carefully</u>, and <u>use the advice</u> you've learnt here. Good luck.

Index